BANNING CONVERSION THERAPY

THE MISSING EVIDENCE

BANNING CONVERSION THERAPY
THE MISSING EVIDENCE

Patricia Morgan

Wilberforce Publications
London

ISBN 978-1-9161211-5-7

Printed in Great Britain by Imprint Digital, Exeter

INTRODUCTION

"The government will ban conversion therapy. There is no justification for these coercive and abhorrent practices and the evidence is clear that it does not work: it does not change a person from being LGBT and can cause long lasting damage to those who go through it." (Banning Conversion Therapy – GOV.UK. 2021)[1]

Such is the confident declaration from a government set on banning the permutations of something otherwise described in terms of "attempts to change, modify or suppress a person's sexual orientation or gender identity". The rhetoric is in inverse proportion to the knowledge of what the target is, let alone the implications of pursuing it.

Policy needs a definable object. This book investigates: what the derogatively titled "coercive and abhorrent practices", or those "attempts to change" might be; if the "evidence is clear" that "it" does not work; and if there is "long lasting damage" for the 'survivors' who have experienced this.

Policy should be based on evidence and awareness of the consequences. With sweeping legal provisos, it is essential to consider the implications for freedom of speech, personal autonomy and parental rights, along with liberty of religion and beliefs – all challenged by claims of "coercive and abhorrent practices".

There is a two-sided endeavour on the part of activists. Measures to change or leave particular identities or tendencies must be forbidden, while processes must be in place for their affirmation. Such ostensibly caring and tolerant objectives have significant totalitarian potential, along with the neglect or encouragement of serious problems particularly affecting youth.

A denial of personal autonomy is more than a matter of protecting people from harms; it is what their participation represents. An ideological imperative targets beliefs conveyed by any "therapeutic approach, or any model or individual viewpoint" which suggests "that any sexual orientation or gender identity is inherently preferable to any other". No judgment must be made or indicated in relation to "all varieties of binary (male or female), non-binary and gender fluid identities".[2]

On its route to legislation, that which is viewed as 'coercive and abhorrent' would go on the back burner before being brought to the fore again. Given the certainties declared and subsequent confusion then, if nothing else, the prospective "conversion therapy" ban provides a test case for the authenticity and legitimacy of Government claims and actions.

CONTENTS

Introduction   5

Chapter One   "Coercive and Abhorrent"   9
1. What is Proposed?   9
2. The Background   17
3. From Torture to Talk   28
4. What is allowed?   45

Chapter Two   Worlds of Fixed and Fluid   63
1. Contrasting perspectives   63

Chapter Three   What to Forbid?   71
1. What is happening?   71
2. Psychiatric practice?   80
3. Self-help?   85
4. Spiritual help?   93

Chapter Four   No Change: Damage Done?   103
1. All decided?   103
2. Difficulties with Damage   118
3. The Most Damaging?   132
4. Change anyway?   145

Chapter Five   A One-Way Ticket   157
1. The Recruiting Drive   157
2. Where Are We Going from Here?   182

Notes   191

Chapter One

"COERCIVE AND ABHORRENT"

1. What is Proposed?

In 2021, the UK Government declared: "We want every individual to have the freedom to be themselves and proposals have been developed with the protection of LGBT people in mind." It was dedicated to "building [a] society in which conversion therapy no longer takes place", with measures "intended to ensure that everyone in this country is protected through both criminal and civil measures". This would include "a new criminal offence" aimed at eradicating the "coercive and abhorrent practice of conversion therapy", or where a person tries to change or suppress a person's sexuality or gender identity, to "ensure that it is stamped out once and for all."[3] The authors of a specialist textbook for psychology courses and lectures state how: "Shockingly, some psychologists and psychiatrists still … advocate the treatment of homosexuality and the use of 'reparative' or 'reorientation' therapy … such terms suggest that the therapist is benevolently helping the client to repair something … which is why we prefer the term 'conversion therapy'. Conversion therapy implies wilfully turning someone from one state to another…".[4]

The ban purports to be "built on a detailed assessment of the existing legislative framework to identify gaps that currently allow conversion therapy to continue", with Government having "analysed the available evidence, listened to stakeholders, [and] learnt from international counterparts …". The proposals are intended to complement increasing bans by the clinical regulatory framework and promise to further "the UK's position as an international leader on LGBT equality, having legalised same-sex marriage and introduced one of the world's most comprehensive legislative frameworks for protecting LGBT people from violence and discrimination". Those who filter the information before presenting it to the Prime Minister may want to ensure that the latter does not become complacent. Organisations such as Stonewall exercise a powerful grip on parliamentary and other leading bodies. As the Government took up transgender ideology, the demands for the legal affirmation of self-defined sexual identity have become increasingly intertwined with calls to ban "conversion therapy".

In 2014, Geraint Davies MP was already pleading with the Parliamentary Under-Secretary of State for Health to "support my Bill to regulate psychotherapists and ban so-called 'gay cures', which cause enormous trauma among their victims".[5] A year on, 12 UN entities were calling on states to end violence towards LGBTQ2+ individuals, including 'abuse in medical settings'.[6] In 2018, Theresa May vowed to eradicate the "abhorrent" practice of gay conversion therapy as she published the world's largest

LGBT+ survey and a government plan aimed at addressing discrimination and health inequality.

With equality achieved on all fronts for LGBTQs, and with Section 28 (which prohibited the promotion of the LGB agenda in schools) long gone, 'change' attempts are providing another adversary for activists to confront. Labour and other parties support a ban, along with tackling more 'hate crime' and 'updating' the Gender Recognition Act to allow for greater self-identification.

The "new criminal offence" would target "conversion therapy" when "committed against under 18s under any circumstance". An adult entering any treatment must prove how they have freely consented, that they have not been influenced by others, and have received all the "information about the potential impacts, short and longer term, of such counselling to allow them to do so; otherwise, this would amount to an offence". In turn, "regulators are best placed to set out professional obligations and identify practices that are harmful for the individual involved".[7] What practices? What harms? Is there a body of knowledge available that fully delineates the nature and extent of the 'damage' or 'harms' rendered by practices which recipients might expect? Otherwise, in the case of a "summary offence" and where the:

> … prosecutor can demonstrate the elements of conversion therapy in court, then the perpetrator may face up to 6 months' imprisonment or a fine of up to an unlimited amount. In cases where the action is tried as an indictable offence and is shown to have seriously harmed the victim (for example, psychiatric

injury), the perpetrator could face imprisonment of up to 5 years.[8]

With claims "that no form of conversion therapy is consistent with the existing regulatory standards of statutory healthcare professionals", there are suggestions that practitioners be disqualified. The police, prosecutors and statutory services are expected to recognise and act on the problem through the development of "new policies". Given what "conversion therapy does to people", the Government will consider, together with support services, how "best to tackle" any promotion or advertisement for any who have been through or are 'at risk' of conversion therapy.

For the Scottish Parliament's Equalities, Human Rights and Civil Justice Committee, the UK government proposals did not go far enough. Tighter and clearer, its report in January 2022 declared:

> … a ban on conversion practices should be fully comprehensive and cover sexual orientation and gender identity, including trans identities, for both adults and children in all settings without exception and include 'consensual' conversion practices.[9]

As there must be a "distinct reporting mechanism for children", would they be encouraged to report their parents or others for not appropriately affirming a new choice of sex or 'gender identity'? What might not have been envisaged is how criminalising any encouragement for gay people to change their sexuality would extend to those expressing an opinion about 'gender identity' or sex-change procedures designed to give effect to a gender identity that is different from the biological one.

The ban raises questions about the ability of parents or others to voice doubts about, or have critical conversations with children pressing for, gender realignment or transition, since this could be breaking the law.

Since consent is irrelevant when it comes to bans on practices like female genital mutilation, forced marriage and honour-based violence, these might be precedents for barring consent as a defence for those who might seek or be undergoing "conversion" practices. The Committee, having "identified gaps that allow other types of conversion therapy to continue", emphasised that any 'talking therapies' within religious settings must "fall within a ban". Consideration must also be "given to providing a separate and distinct reporting mechanism for children" to report possible offenders. At the same time, 'affirmative therapies' for sexual orientation and gender identity "should be protected under any ban".[10] Actually, affirmative help or supportive services are available and recommended by the NHS, from Mind LGBTIQ+ to Gendered Intelligence to Pink Therapy to Stonewall to Imaan (for Muslim LGBTQs) and many others.[11] The influential American Psychological Association's 'Task Force on Guidelines for Psychological Practice with Transgender and Gender Nonconforming People (TGNC)' insists that psychologists and other professional counsellors offer "trans-affirmative" care. This extends to displaying "TGNC-affirmative resources in waiting areas" and practitioners using transgender appropriate language to make patients feel supported.

Then there is the wide-ranging 'LGBTQ+ Action Plan for Wales', heavily influenced by Stonewall and other LGBT organisations. The goals, along with banning "all aspects of LGBTQ+ conversion therapy", aim to challenge "heteronormative and cisnormative assumptions", not least that there are biological sexes.[12] This relates to how the existence of conversion therapy in any form is seen as an endorsement of biases against homosexuality, as much as it confirms the perceived self-hatred of those seeking an alleged cure.

The UK Government advertised a contract to set up a Conversion Therapy Victims' Helpline or Service in advance of its bill.[13] This would direct people to other, "relevant services" – or bring services to them – and provide "support to individuals who have gone through, are going through, or are at risk of, conversion therapy practices" and provide "public information" about this. Those "relevant services" include counselling, making reports to the police and providing emergency housing, as well as helping anybody aware of instances of 'conversion therapy' about what action to take. Under this proposal, members of the public or colleagues can put others under investigation by reporting a "risk of conversion therapy".

A person "who has had or is at risk" of "conversion therapy" would be able to apply for a Protection Order from courts, which suggests that being a 'victim' could be more or less self-defined. Such subjectivity appears to be comparable with the current processes for registering a 'hate crime' or 'hate incident'. It has been suggested that family courts should also be empowered to use Conversion Therapy Protection Orders to stop parents allowing children to undergo this "abusive practice",

with a mandatory legal requirement to report suspected cases.

There may well be parents who take a principled
stance with sexuality or gender non-conforming
youngsters.[14] It is claimed that over-reaction, along with
rejection, can cause conflict and all manner of problems
from depression to drug-use, to running away and
perhaps embed what it was meant to reduce. However,
with suggestions of criminalising anything less than the
speedy full endorsement of another's minority sexual or
gender identity, a comprehensive 'conversion' ban might
well stretch to those unsupportive or neutral over a
transgender or same-sex identification.

"Conversion therapy" may cover "any approach that
aims to persuade 'trans' people to accept their sex
assigned at birth" or "placing barriers [to] medical
transition". Given the enormous increase in adolescents
with gender dysphoria, this might apply to trying to
prevent youngsters taking 'sex swap' drugs, or puberty-
blockers and cross-sex hormones to transition to the
opposite gender. When children are said to 'know who
they are', this is already discrimination based on their
'transgender identity'. A question is whether, alongside
Protection Orders, risk assessments would be available
under existing law (Children Act 1989) to enable
children to be removed from families when reports of
exposure to 'conversion therapy' are made?

More comprehensive suggestions include obligations
on statutory services "to develop policy frameworks that
recognise conversion therapy as a problem ... and to
provide training for how to protect people from these

practices" in line with clinical regulations. To this end the "government will work with the relevant public authorities in order to develop this guidance". A question is whether LGBT organisations would operate throughout social services on the government's behalf to design procedures in parallel with their work to promote the LGBT agenda throughout education. Would these be directing actual or possible victims to "relevant, existing services" or their own affirmative services – including 'pastoral support' from pro-LGBT religious and other organisations?

Broader still, the government has aimed to share its work to ban conversion therapy "with all our international counterparts", promising to "work with partners to end these practices across the world". The official website of the Office of the High Commissioner of the United Nations Human Rights organisation described how a UN expert calling for a global ban had told the Human Rights Council: "Practices known as 'conversion therapy' inflict severe pain and suffering on lesbian, gay, bisexual, trans and gender-diverse (LGBT) persons, often resulting in long-lasting psychological and physical damage…".[15] To secure comprehensive legislative bans, Victor Madrigal-Borloz, the UN LGBT 'czar', had been collecting worldwide evidence to prove how the variants of 'conversion therapy' could be universally categorised as 'torture'.[16]

2. The Background

As part of "the duty of the government to keep its citizens safe", the proposals to ban 'conversion therapy' or "ending the coercive and abhorrent practice" were speedily launched with a six-week consultation for closure in December 2021, along with promises to put legislation on the statute book by May 2022. Claims are that the consultation period was halved from the normal 12 weeks to get a 'good news story' flagged up about the legal ban in time for the Government's *Safe To Be Me: A Global Equality Conference*' in June, to coincide with the 50th anniversary of the first official London Pride marches. This optimistic timescale was amended to the standard 12-week consultation period after threats of legal action from *Fair Play For Women*, worried how a ban would consolidate the 'affirm and transition' approach for gender-dysphoric children. This was further extended to 14 weeks. The three-day conference was to highlight discrimination against gay and transgender people and develop policies to safeguard them. Lord Herbert of South Downs, a Tory peer, was handed £8m to promote the conference across the world with visits from Mexico to Malta to Argentina. He proposed inviting US vice president Kamala Harris and Canadian Prime Minister Justin Trudeau as speakers; their security would cost £3m. The conference was subsequently cancelled.

The consultation would subsequently fail to impress the Equality and Human Rights Commission, which by early 2022 ceased to be a Stonewall 'diversity champion'. In its response on Banning Conversion Therapy, it rather derisibly observed that a "more robust" result "would have been achieved had additional information been provided on the definition of the key concepts of "conversion therapy" and "transgender". As it would remind advocates, you cannot "legislate without definitions or evidence".[17] Without "a clear legal definition of what is meant by conversion therapy", it was "concerned that the information in this consultation provides insufficient detail to enable us or the public to provide a sufficiently informed response."

Nothing like this seemed to have occurred to Baroness Helena Kennedy, who condemned any consultation and demanded that the government "implement this legislation without delay ... too many lives have already been affected by this form of abuse and countless more are still at risk".[18] Alicia Kearns, a Tory MP, claimed (in 2021) how she came into Parliament with this "one legislative change I wanted to deliver, which was to ban conversion therapy". Irrespective of whether this was why the constituents elected her, she wants criminalisation of those who "force" someone to undergo 'conversion therapy', along with any who "aid and procure these abusive services to repress or eliminate a person's sexual orientation or manifestation of that sexual orientation". A ban must include "attempts to prevent, against the individual's wishes, a gender transition", with Kearns simultaneously speaking of prosecuting: "those responsible (especially for non-violent practices) ..." or those practising talking therapies, *together* with those administering electric shocks and enforced confinement.[19] Indeed, since GBH

(Grievous Bodily Harm) law does not apply to counselling, she wants legislation to "give survivors [sic] the ability to prosecute those responsible (especially for non-violent practices) ... and create a strong deterrent in law".[20]

Kearns ascribes her inspiration for this policy initiative to seeing "on the eve of LGBTQ+ History Month, *It's A Sin* premiered on our screens". This is "haunting and heart-breaking ... laying bare the trauma inflicted by prejudice, ignorance and frankly, hatred, on the lives of a group of gay men and their loved ones" back during the 1980s' experience with AIDs. This series, which so mesmerised Kearns, is reported as having an approval rating of 100% with "an exquisite [sic] cast, empathetic writing, and a distinct visual style ... an incredible feat of small-screen magic".[21] Moreover, as reported:

> It is not however a story of discrimination long-since exorcised from our society. Thousands of LGBTQ+ people are subject to trauma every day. Nowhere is this more evident than in the fraudulent and abhorrent practice of LGBTQ+ conversion therapy, which Roscoe flees home to escape at the beginning of the TV series.[22]

Thousands traumatised every day? Among the 'evidence' of so many terrible accounts is an op-ed by Sam Brinton run by The *New York Times* (January 2018) under the headline, "Tortured in Gay Conversion Therapy." (The online version adds: "And It's Still Legal in 41 States.")[23] The therapist allegedly tied the victim to a table and applied ice, heat and electricity to his body as he was forced to watch clips of men having gay sex. There has, however, been no identification of the counsellor allegedly engaged in such practices or where this might have happened, casting doubts on its authenticity.

Another emotive composition is *The Miseducation of Cameron Post*, a "brilliant conversion drama", about a US school where gay teenagers are tortured to turn them straight, with bizarre but futile "bless-a-cis" workouts and group confessions. This is based on a novel, although reviewers have suggested that it actually happened. One in *The New York Times* wanted "to wish for an angrier, more pointed critique of [the fictional therapy] and the religious point of view it represents".[24]

Following on is the gay film *Boy Erased*, where Jared is sent to a conversion camp where he is force-fed hard-line Christianity to 'cure' his homosexual 'leanings'.[25] In The *Guardian*, Baroness Helena Kennedy talks of how these "practices cause untold harm to millions of LGBT+ people" and lead "many to believe the only way to deal with their psychological trauma and shame is to take their lives."[26] As she has seen "LGBT+ people being prayed for at 'ex-gay' conferences … in the Netflix drama, *Pray Away*", she wants all religious procedures to "face the full force of the law" including any "one-to-one ministry sessions". Untold harm to millions and mass suicide?

Transgender's rise to prominence is accompanied by accounts such as one from a transgender person about being tortured at an Ohio-based 'conversion therapy' camp in 2019. In the film *True*, victims claimed to have been repeatedly hooked up to electrodes and given forced IV injections to vomit uncontrollably, while being made to watch negative images. According to the office of the Ohio Secretary of State and Attorney General, no such camp ever existed. The only trace is to a 1999 film *But I'm a Cheerleader*.[27]

Activists hope that horrific accounts "will help to spur politicians to ban this practice". Re-named 'conversion abuse' this, "shockingly, is claimed to be thriving here" according to *Stories of Our Times: Thinking Straight* (Times Radio, Apple, Spotify, et al).[28] Media dramas seem to be where Baroness Williams of Trafford also gets her information from when she emphasises how the government "plans to ban it for adults and especially for children". Speaking at the Government Equalities Office's [GEO] LGBT Leadership Summit, she had been:

> … absolutely shocked that this is practised at all in the modern world. The techniques employed by people who promote these practices are quite frightening and have very tragic consequences in many cases. LGBT people are not broken, they're not ill, they don't need to be fixed and they don't need to be cured. And that's why the government is committed to ending these practices for good.[29]

Proponents of conversion therapy bans are not alone in using poignant images and shocking claims to further legislative and other moves. In themselves, these cannot signify the desirability or otherwise of any proposals, or even the authenticity of the material being presented as evidence. In the 'heart-breaking' film *Vera Drake*, there is the perpetually teary-eyed, devoted wife and mother. A persecuted backstreet abortionist, she speechlessly faces the force of law for kindly helping desperate local women. Rapid media expansion has meant that more and more dramatic representations can now further a cause, irrespective of the evidence.

The 12-person LGBT advisory panel set up by the Government in 2018 was conveniently placed for driving plans for "ending the practice of conversion therapy in the UK" – outlined in the *LGBT Action Plan 2018*.[30] This followed a national survey in 2017 open to those who identified as having a minority sexual orientation, gender identity or variations in sexual characteristics. The 108,000 respondents were asked questions about living in the UK and in accessing public services.

Fronted by Penny Mordaunt MP, then Minister for Women and Equalities, other 'key actions' are: "Appointing a national LGBT health adviser to provide leadership on reducing the health inequalities that LGBT people face; Extending the anti-homophobic, biphobic and transphobic bullying programme in schools; Taking further action on LGBT hate crime – improving the recording and reporting of, and police response to, hate crime." There would be £4.5m "to deliver commitments" through an 'LGBT Implementation Fund'" for "public, private and voluntary sector organisations to deliver projects to support LGBT people".

With "additional funding after March 2020", the GEO would "work with other departments and LGBT sector organisations to build a business case for further investment in initiatives to improve outcomes for LGBT people." Ensuring that "LGBT people's needs are at the heart of the National Health Service" will "enhance fertility services for LGBT people" as the Department for Health and Social Care "revises surrogacy legislation for single people (including LGBT individuals)". The Department for Education has £2m to "establish regional hubs to support teachers from under-represented groups" like LGBTs "to progress into leadership." A £3m programme for schools to tackle "antihomophobic, biphobic and transphobic bullying" will be followed by more in 2019/2020 to also cover further and higher education institutions. The £96m for the Ministry of Justice, ostensibly to increase public safety and support victims of crime, included "specific projects for LGBT victims" to build on those established in previous years.

All added to pressure for outlawing any forms of counselling or persuasion to change sexual orientation or behaviour to conform to a 'heteronormative' lifestyle, or anything that discouraged 'identity change' or non-recognition of 'gender choice', no matter the age or the reason, religious or otherwise. As the GEO – based at the Cabinet Office, then a member of Stonewall's Diversity Champions scheme – was not willing to let such activities continue, it promised to fully consider all legislative and non-legislative options to prohibit promoting, offering, or conducting 'conversion therapy'. It had the backing of the Equality and Human Rights Commission, then led by David Isaac, previously the chair of Stonewall.

There was a parliamentary debate about a ban prompted by a petition which, having passed 100,000 signatures, had to be considered. It took place in Westminster Hall, where petition debates allow all party MPs to discuss particular issues and put their concerns to

Government, while obviating any vote leading to legislation.

Disregarding the fact that the Petitions Committee has a right to request a debate, activists emphatically did not want divergent opinions to be aired in any publicly exposed setting. The House of Commons Twitter account had previously tweeted a survey asking how conversion therapy affected the LGBTQ community: "Should it be made illegal?"; "What would that mean to you?"[31] Enraged activists demanded deletion for suggesting that a ban could ever be a matter for debate. It was "insane", "outrageous" and "insensitive" that such questions be asked. Shadow Foreign Office and Development minister Stephen Doughty raised concerns about this "inappropriate and insensitive" tweet with the House of Commons Petitions Committee. The lobby group titled 'Gendered Intelligence', asked if torture against minorities should be made illegal or just continue as it is. Labour MP Stella Creasy added: "What would it mean to me if we made sure torture was illegal in our own country that we challenge in others?"

For Laura Russell from Stonewall: "Any form of 'therapy' that attempts to change someone's sexual orientation or gender identity is unethical and wrong", since a "person's sexual orientation and gender identity is a natural, normal part of their identity and not something that can or should be changed". For her, these "conversion therapies have been condemned by all major UK health organisations as these practices try to shame a person into denying a core part of who they are and this can have a seriously damaging effect on their mental health and wellbeing". Her view is that the Government should "hold true to their commitment to end this harmful practice, once and for all".[32] Transgender model Munroe Bergdorf, known for her opinion that "all white people are racist", cried: "This is outrageous. Conversion Therapy is not a debate. Shut it down."[33]

The House of Commons Twitter account deleted the call for opinions and humbly apologised "to anyone who was offended by our post. Our intention was to provide a platform for people to share their opinions on this important subject with the Petitions Committee and inform its case to the Government." This ignored how any bill may have to undergo parliamentary debate. Activists were demanding that something be banned, but without explaining and arguing why, or even properly defining what the target was. They were, effectively, calling for a subversion of democratic procedures. This suggests moves to introduce gender self-affirmation legislation by subterfuge.[34]

There was no dissenting voice at the Westminster Petitions Committee discussion, where MPs competed "to express their horror at gay and trans people being subjected to this practice".[35] Kemi Badenoch, the Women and Equalities Minister, was criticised for not using the word 'banned' sufficiently and referring to legislation already in place. She emphasised the government's commitment to ensuring all citizens feel safe and protected from harm, and building a country in which everyone, "no matter their sexuality, race or religion, is free to live their lives as they choose". Overlooked might be how, with a comprehensive conversion therapy ban in place, some might be unable to "live their lives as they choose".

In early 2021, the Government's LGBT advisory panel had three resignations, ostensibly because of the delays in banning 'conversion therapy' – although the members' terms were soon due to end.[36] After leading activist Jayne Ozanne quit, she was followed by James Morton and Ellen Murray, disappointed by the government's approach to transgender rights and "hostility" towards LGBT people. Hitting out at Liz Truss and Kemi Badenoch, Ozanne called them "ministers for inequality" and got nearly 20 LGBT organisations (and Peter Tatchell) to express "deep concern" at their inaction. Nancy Kelley, chief executive of Stonewall, a remaining LGBT panel member, said: "Many key commitments from the UK LGBT Action Plan remain incomplete, including delivering an effective ban on conversion therapy, and the pandemic has only deepened the inequalities LGBTQ people experience, particularly in mental health."[37]

The LGBT panel may not have received the attention its creation promised. Ozanne complained that ministers had shown a lack of action and engagement with their advice. The panel felt that the "government does not seem … to have any desire to build a country in which trans people are among those free to live their lives". Compared with the previous government, where members (including the Prime Minister, Theresa May) were much more LGBT-allied, drift seemed to be underway.

Under pressure from LGBT groups, Prime Minister Boris Johnson "repeatedly made clear that we will take action to end conversion therapy and we are working to bring forward plans to do so shortly".[38] Welcoming Johnson's promise, Ozanne hoped that it would "protect … particularly trans people who are the most at risk".[39] The LGBT advisory panel was disbanded in April 2021, with promises that a replacement "will be set out in due course". Minister Liz Truss announced the inauguration of the International LGBT Conference and how the government was "convening a new body that will take international LGBT rights forward". She would be "pressing ahead with our commitment to ban conversion therapy … to protect LGBT people from these abhorrent practices". Others detected equivocation as Truss defended single-sex spaces out of concern for women's rights.

On behalf of the Evangelical Alliance, director Peter Lynas wrote in March 2021 to Boris Johnson, asking him to clarify what a ban might mean for the everyday activities of UK churches and Christians, not least in terms of transmitting biblical beliefs relating to marriage and sexuality or what would be defined as 'conversion therapy'. Johnson claimed to "take freedom of speech and freedom of religion very seriously". Adults would be allowed to "receive appropriate pastoral support (including prayer), in churches and other religious settings, in the exploration of their sexual orientation or gender identity. … I do not want to see clergy and church members criminalised for normal non-coercive activity." This provoked outrage.

Campaigners renewed their pressure to ban 'barbaric' conversion therapy after a Stormont minister vowed to bring in legislation against anything which "falsely" claims to change a person's sexual orientation or gender identity "in all its forms". In the May 2021 Queen's Speech, the UK Government then committed to introducing legislation to ban an 'abhorrent' practice based on beliefs that being lesbian, gay, bisexual or transgender is a mental illness that can be 'cured'. This made an appearance the following year.

3. From Torture to Talk

The "phrase 'conversion therapy' has conjured up images of quack faith healers shrieking and wielding electrodes – images reinforced with regular references to 'abhorrent practices' (a phrase used twelve times in the Westminster Hall debate…)".[40] Repeated across media is how there can be no debate on 'so-called' conversion therapy, any more than on public flogging, torture or FGM. In 2021, Janice Turner in *The Times* tells of:

> Young men forced to sit through slideshows strapped with electrodes, receiving vicious shocks if they dwelled on images of men. Lesbians were "cured" of their urges via "corrective" rape. Aged 17, the US writer Andrew Solomon saw a female "sex surrogate" to learn heterosexual ways. Christians, Muslims, Sikhs and Jews have suffered disturbing exorcisms to "pray away the gay".[41]

There might be analogies here to accounts of children being raped and sacrificed on pagan alters by politicians, or the kind of accusations made in historic witch crazes. With the 'relevant services' proposed for those exposed to 'conversion therapy' to include police protection and emergency housing, this suggests victims fleeing from fanatical gangs or family jailers.

Conspiracy theories might be expected. A medical source speaks of how even the term 'conversion therapy' is a 're-labelling' or part of attempts to disguise what is really 'aversion therapy', including electroconvulsive therapy. Cast as primarily "shepherded through religious ex-gay institutions", this is described as a "dangerous practice of forcing individuals to conform to the heterosexual and cisgender normative expectation" and while "ineffective, and often harmful, it is still being used in 2022", resulting in "a myriad of psychopathologic conditions". It is lamented that, while the "human toll is unimaginable" this is still not "high enough for the practice to be thoroughly banned ...".[42]

It is also claimed that acquaintance with the economic costs might help, with estimates of total lifetime excess costs of $83,366 per US individual at risk from SOGICE (sexual orientation and gender identity change efforts). This is primarily attributed to suicidality, anxiety, severe psychological distress, depression, and substance abuse (calculated from worse case scenarios). Or, for 4,554,300 LGBTQ youths (10% of their population), this translates to total costs of over $650m for SOGICE in 2021, with harms associated with an estimated economic burden of $9.23 billion for an "unnecessary, harmful practice".[43] It is hoped that, made aware of the economic cost, "humanity might redirect its reparative efforts toward dismantling the harmful hetero and cisgender normative chokehold that continues to asphyxiate social evolution".[44]

Legislative measures have clearly been advanced amid great sound and fury, with terms such as 'damage', 'harm' and 'trauma' continually reiterated when, despite the claims, there are no court cases where a licensed professional has been found to have used torture or been abusive when dealing with unwanted same-sex attraction or gender discordance. While many are held to be at great 'risk of conversion therapy', there is little information for the actual threats they face or what the reality of the nightmarish "coercive and abhorrent" practices might be. Presenting the ban, the government repeats the rhetoric that:

> There is no justification for these coercive and abhorrent practices and the evidence is clear that it does not work: it does not change a person from being LGBT and can cause lasting damage to those who go through it. [45]

How? It is unknown how many victims are out there or what 'long lasting damage' they have suffered. As an empirically minded researcher concludes, "it is difficult to estimate the true prevalence of conversion therapy among LGBT people in the general population". [46]

The term 'conversion' may be referring to what has been variously called 'change' therapy, 'reparative' therapy or SOCE (sexual orientation change efforts), coined by the American Psychological Association as a generic term for all change-oriented procedures. This description was to put down what are considered directive approaches and extends beyond professionally conducted therapy to include all manner of counselling and other interventions. The implication is that categorical change (from exclusive same-sex attraction or identity to opposite-sex attraction or identity) is the expected goal, when this is statistically rare for any genuine psychological procedure. The UK's International Federation for Therapeutic and Counselling Choice was set up to counter prohibitions on help for those seeking changes in same-sex attractions and behaviours, or deal with unwanted feelings and confusions, and sees this labelling as having been developed to disparage its practice, which it prefers to call SAFE-T or Sexual Attraction Fluidity Exploration in Therapy.[47] Elsewhere, "the umbrella term 'affectional reorientation therapy' describes efforts to change one's attractions to individuals of the same sex" through different psychotherapeutic or clinical techniques.[48]

As variants of 'talk therapy' are the real issue here, it might seem hyperbolic to suggest that special counselling, police reports and emergency housing are necessary when the only possible 'peril' to be addressed is no more than psychotherapy. Questions might be labelled as insensitive amid all the outrage, where the momentum is sustained by references which slide from torture to conversation and from coercion to consent and back again.

With persistent accounts of atrocious abuse, *The Daily Mail* still proclaimed in 2021: "Scarred by the gay conversion zealots: Electrocuted, exorcised, and beaten. As a new law is unveiled to outlaw barbaric 'therapy' to make gay people straight, four victims bravely tell of their experiences."[49] This picks up on a lead in 2019, which spoke of "hypnosis and electric shocks ..." and referenced "the International Lesbian, Gay, Bisexual, Trans and Intersex Association (ILGA), a network of LGBTQ+ groups". Thus, even if "conversion therapy sounds like something from a bygone age or a practice that could only be allowed in a more oppressive, less tolerant nation, it is alive and well in the UK today".[50] But where is this happening?

The Daily Mail previously highlighted a Channel 4 documentary series, *Cure Me, I'm Gay* by Christian Jessen, a celebrity TV doctor who presented *Embarrassing Bodies*. He would test "a series of controversial therapies for 'curing' homosexuality". (Anybody doing this, who is reputedly versed in the gay sex scene, might resemble a committed alcoholic out to prove that Alcoholics Anonymous doesn't work). Presented as "advocated predominantly by right-wing fundamentalist American religious organisations and groups such as the National Association for Research and Therapy of Homosexuality (NARTH)", these covered "electric shock therapy, inducing nausea while being exposed to homoerotic material, praying, exorcism, trips to brothels to have sex with women, and hypnosis". There is a retro photo of somebody strapped down with his head held in something resembling a giant vice.[51]

If this is supposed to be present reality, a ready solution to 'conversion therapy' could be to ban any violent and coercive procedures. Existing laws criminalise physical and sexual assault, threats, verbal abuse and enforced confinement – although, as with any violence or force, not all instances can be prevented or detected. Those who repeat emotive stories of electrocution and rape, including MPs, "seemed to be forgetting that it is already illegal to physically harm people in the UK or to exercise coercive control."[52]

The Government admits "that conversion therapy amounting to offences of physical or sexual violence is already illegal in this country". However, further legislation will "ensure this sinister motivation for violence is considered by the judge as a potential aggravating factor upon sentencing", when there are already heavier penalties for assaults on those with 'protected characteristics', which might qualify as 'hate crime'.[53] A question could be why a "sinister motivation" for assaults on some people merits higher penalties than violence against others?

There might be thought to be no one better placed to speak of alleged horrors than Jayne Ozanne.[54] She is referenced as the Scottish Parliament's Equalities, Human Rights and Civil Justice Committee's leading authority on the practice and effects of conversion therapy.[55]

As a prominent gay activist in the Church of England, Ozanne rose to fame with her story of how 'spiritual abuse' in a charismatic evangelical church led to her having one or two or more (reports vary) nervous breakdowns. Unless this was banned, high rates of suicide, self-harm and depression among LGBTQ Christians would continue unabated, when it was necessary to "celebrate who we are". Presenting a motion to the Church of England Synod in 2017, Ozanne and the Oasis Foundation urged all churches and the government to impose a comprehensive ban on anything – religious or lay – aimed at changing sexual preferences as forms of abuse directed at "vulnerable adults and children", along with the abandonment of "negative views to debates about same-sex relationships …". The Synod agreed.

Ozanne claims that there are "tens of thousands of people in the UK who have endured this. I know of at least a thousand myself", along with extreme forms of therapy involving "exorcisms, physical violence and food deprivation. It's happening every day in leafy suburbs [sic] and university cities. I got off lightly. I'm aware of others who have been raped, electrocuted, violently beaten or burnt." (Are there any police or medical records?) Her experience with a "therapy session", took place in "a cosy suburban sitting room" with somebody described as a "female therapist" and "faith leader" who, for five hours, urged her to vomit out her attraction to women. As if she had "survived a terrible crash … delicate veins around her eyes ruptured, she had to wear sunglasses for a week, unable to bear daylight". She claims to have endured these sessions for 20 years (?) and went to meetings where strangers "shouted to rid me of the evil inside me". At one, a leader placed his hands on her shoulders and "commanded the spirit of lust to leave me", she says, shuddering at the memory.

Did Ozanne have to go to 'spiritual healing'? Was her breakdown solely due to this or were there other underlying or contributory causes? Should one person's accounts of grief malign and forbid any manner of interventions, secular and religious, of another individual's choosing?

Was it endured by tens of thousands? The Cooper Report commissioned by the Ozanne Foundation, or *How to Legislate against Conversion Practices*, was signed off by a Forum of 17 chaired by Baroness Kennedy. These included Susie Green from Mermaids, Peter Tatchell, Nancy Kelley from Stonewall, Jayne Ozanne, a selection of MPs including Angela Eagle (Labour), Crispin Blunt (Chair of APPG on Global LGBT Rights) and various professors. This declared:

> ... in addition to a general offence prohibiting all forms of conversion practices, statutory provisions are also adopted to ensure a comprehensive ban. These should include banning the promotion or advertising of conversion practices ... engaging in conversion practices should be an aggravating factor in sentencing where existing criminal offences are involved. ... restrictions on the right to manifest religion and belief and their expression, which are necessary, justified and proportionate under Articles 9 and 10 ECHR. An exemption for religious conversion practices, such as an act of spoken prayer directed at an individual with the predetermined purpose of suppressing, curing or changing their sexual orientation or gender identity, would undermine the efficacy of the prohibition.

Moreover:

> For the same reason, there can be no exemptions for 'consenting' adults who seek out conversion practices despite the harm involved. This is because the pressures and imbalance of power involved mean that such 'consent' cannot be truly free or autonomously exercised. Allowing these to continue would put a significant number of vulnerable people at risk.[56]

Along with the Scottish Parliament's suggestions, there are calls for "providing a separate and distinct reporting mechanism for children", given how parents may have "the directed intent to change their child's sexuality or gender identity".

An earlier survey of faith and sexuality, organised by Ozanne's foundation, found "that 22 participants said they had undergone forced sexual activity with, or involving, someone of the opposite gender". She further claims that other surveys (without reference) on faith and sexuality have found that 10% of those that took part had undergone efforts to change their sexuality, with one in ten saying they had no choice about this. The "reported" mental health problems attributed to experiences with 'conversion therapy' are anxiety and depression, suicidal thoughts or attempts, self-harming and eating disorders.[57] The LGBT charity, Galop, adds that:

> We see young people, including under-18s, who have been victims of serious psychological, sexual and physical abuse in the attempt to change who they are ...

> Some are faced with forced marriage or abduction. Others have sustained physical trauma so serious they needed to be hospitalised.[58]

Alicia Kearns MP re-emphasised how "attempts to use medical, psychological and social methods to 'convert' someone away from their innate sexual orientation" range "from 'therapy' and prayer sessions, to ... electroshocks or even 'corrective' rape". All are "deeply harmful, causing life-long difficulties in forming relationships, experiencing positive emotions and main-

taining self-esteem along with the painful physical man-
ifestations of abuse".[59]

A critic might see every shibboleth present in
sensationalised accounts, with even 'tens of thousands'
being coerced in facilities suggesting Soviet Gulags or
Maoist re-education camps. Emotive anecdotes are
repeated and worked-up for maximum effect, but reality
checks are missing. For activists, any 'change therapy' is
an invariably appalling practice, with such 'damaging'
consequences that the victims end up in hospital, if they
don't try suicide first. It is not callous to ask for evidence,
such as: "for what and where were any hospitalised?"

Many torture accounts come from the US, with
Hollywood helping SOCE to be accepted as dangerous
and fraudulent by the US's most prominent medical
and mental health professional organisations, including
the American Medical Association, the American
Psychiatric Association, and the American Psychological
Association.[60] Representatives from gay and human
rights organizations and mental health associations
have testified about the dangers. Others, like the
Southern Poverty Law Center (SPLC), a wealthy,
aggressively left-wing, anti-Christian political group,
have sued purportedly SOCE providers (using charges
of fraud under consumer protection laws). By 2021,
there were bans on SOCE in place in 28 states and the
District of Columbia. These might include consumer
rights provisions, since providers' change therapies may
be construed as committing 'consumer fraud,' on the
basis that their 'damaging' practices do not work.

When Penny Mordaunt was UK Minister for Equalities, the Government Equalities Office reiterated claims about 'corrective rape' as a form of 'conversion therapy', which resulted in two Freedom of Information requests asking for supporting evidence. The civil servants for the Government Equalities Office (GEO) denied that they had made the association. Yet, in its National LGBT Survey, the GEO said: "We did not provide a definition of conversion therapy in the survey, but it can range from pseudo-psychological treatments to, in extreme cases, surgical interventions and 'corrective' rape." [61] But where was the evidence for this?

The GEO commissioned research from Coventry University (a Stonewall Diversity Champion) in advance of a 'conversion therapy' ban. Appearing in late 2021, this was meant to inform policy development on the practice of 'conversion therapy' and the options for ending this in the UK. Despite the researchers' support for comprehensive bans, no 'aversive' techniques were reported by their self-selected interviewees, apart from one transgender respondent claiming to have been shown a video of gender reassignment surgery.[62]

A previous study of the circumstances since the 1950s – in which those attracted to the same sex were subjected to efforts to change their sexuality – used a volunteer sample of 29 people who were in their late teens and early twenties when they underwent these measures. There was a complex of social and personal along with medical and legal reasons for participation, which peaked in the early 1960s when homosexuality was seen as a mental illness. What passed for psychiatry involved either psychoanalysis or behavioural aversion therapy with electric shocks, between the 1960s and early 1970s (with nausea caused by the drug apomorphine affecting four people in the early 1960s), although none was lengthy or extensive.[63] In those times ECT was also used for depression and even high blood pressure.

For these cases, there were no effects in terms of orientation changes; many retained a sense of unease about their sexuality, and a few were enabled to accept this. General outcomes cannot be known since the participants were not representative of those who underwent treatment. The BBC News website's *Family & Education* section recently carried a story about a man demanding an apology from Birmingham University for giving him electric shock treatment for homosexuality over fifty years ago.[64] As if this operated today, Ben Hunte, the BBC News LGBT Correspondent, urged the Government to hurry with plans to ban 'conversion therapy'. Is it on the basis of these historical references that Boris Johnson labelled the practice "absolutely abhorrent" with "no place in a civilised society"?[65]

There is a 'straw man' argument here. 'Coercive and abhorrent' practices, like the 'forcible administration' of ECT for same-sex attraction or gender dysphoria, are long abandoned or renounced by UK mental health bodies. Evidence has not been produced for contemporary practitioners doing what identity groups and the media have alleged about 'conversion' torture. It is always possible that cases could emerge, as for instances of other awful happenings. So far, none in the UK appear to be being beaten, raped, electrocuted, burnt, imprisoned or lobotomised to convert from homo/bisexual to heterosexual, or return to their natal sex identity, although increasingly of late, information may have been somewhat scarce. With the removal of homosexuality as a mental disorder from the Diagnostic and Statistical Manual of Mental Disorders (1987), studies of therapies aimed at changing sexual orientation or behaviour were often abandoned for ethical and legal reasons, while the remaining therapeutic interventions became more affirmative of same-sex and transgender identifications.

Should images conjured out of the air, and hyped-up media accounts or films replete with sensational and emotive imagery, be taken for reality, or treated as trustworthy sources of factual information? Should these, along with activists' hyperbolic language, shape attitudes and approaches to controversial issues? Should these be uncritically accepted as worthy bases for policy and law making, determining the decisions of politicians and professionals? To profess abhorrence with alleged practices might appear to demonstrate someone's credentials, but the truth is that the practices are unlikely to exist any longer. That legislation can be proposed by the Government based on false premises and the absence of evidence is very worrying.

While the 'stop torturing' call raises support, concentrating on matters like electrocution would make a legal ban confined only to such activities pointless if there are no verifiable instances. Douglas Murray asked, when the nation was facing "some very real perils" in the early 2020s, how can a "phantom in retreat ... be among their legislative priorities"?[66] If this was really the advocates' primary or only target, the cause would collapse. Indeed, Ozanne and other campaigners fear there is a risk of a "highly dangerous loophole" being created if the Government focused only on "coercive practices" rather than "all forms of conversion therapy, to which vulnerable victims may willingly submit" or agree to. [67]

That last sentence is telling. Along with being held down, electrocuted and raped, references to 'abhorrent and coercive practices' are used to include all forms of 'conversion' which comprise any assistance anyone might seek in order to live in the manner that they choose, such as to help to reduce or leave same- or both-sex- attractions or behaviour, or to identify with their natal sex. Advocates envisage a ban covering all healthcare provisions along with religious, cultural and traditional interventions, whether coercive or consensual, big or small, for minors and adults. A ban on matters like electrocution would have none of the far-reaching social impacts that activists are campaigning for.

The investigation commissioned by the GEO from Coventry University ignored the accounts of electrocution and rape, probably aware that something with no existence outside of media would effectively make prohibition pointless. Described instead is how the "most common methods identified involved a combination of spiritual (e.g. prayer 'healing'/exorcisms/pastoral counselling) and psychological methods (e.g. talking therapies), with "boundaries between religious and psychological approaches ... often unclear with many combining the two ...". Conversion therapy can "refer to any efforts to change, modify or suppress a person's sexual orientation or gender identity irrespective of whether it takes place in healthcare, religious or other settings".[68]

Therapies for anything are generally sought and agreed by the client, and these could hardly be effective were it otherwise. People are not normally forced to undergo any treatment they do not want and again, there are existing provisions to deal with coercive extremes, even if these may sometimes pass detection. Otherwise, what are essentially voluntary talking procedures or counselling are usually something clients want and are willing to cooperate with. Therapy cannot be successful if forced or involuntarily imposed: involuntary therapy is invariably failed therapy.

However, when all discussion, advice or treatment is alleged to cause 'damage', the argument is that no one should be able to consent to any form of 'change' therapy, and that there should be a statutory duty to intervene and overrule people's choices. Jayne Ozanne insists in *The Guardian* how the UK must ban 'conversion therapy' – "even for adults who claim to want it", if it is to make any sense at all. Her recommendations are reflected in official banning plans, like those of the Equalities, Human Rights and Civil Justice Committee of the Scottish Parliament.[69] The ambitious plans of influential Canadian LGBT activist Kristopher Wells (Research Chair for the Public Understanding of Sexual and Gender Minority Youth at MacEwan University, Alberta), and Nicholas Schiavo of *No Conversion Canada* would ban any 'treatment' which questions or attempts to change someone's sexual orientation, gender identity or expression. This comprehensively covers individual talk therapy, behaviour therapy, group therapy, spiritual prayer and/or medical or drug-related treatments.[70]

There are claims that LGBT individuals suffer heightened levels of psychological distress attributable to internalised prejudice and discrimination. When these people seek therapy, hoping to overcome negative feelings about their sexual orientation, they are regarded as adding further risks to their mental health and wellbeing by internalising the stigmatisation and rejection that they are already receiving from society.

Where the very desire to change sexual orientation is seen as a reflection of oppression since this is not accepted as voluntary and so for the victim's own good, it cannot be allowed. It might look as if change seekers are being grouped together with the insane or that, incapable of rational decisions, they are simply passive victims who cannot control their lives. This does not respect their rights, self-determination or autonomy.[71]

All this signifies how those who seek change are deemed to embody or represent unacceptable beliefs. This is irrespective of what the individual may think or believe about sexual orientations or gender identities when personally seeking to leave unwanted predispositions, tendencies or habits, or what may be practitioners' responses to various problems or mental conditions. Essentially, conformity to ideology is compulsory and usurps individual autonomy and freedom of choice. The 2022 Memorandum of Understanding (MoU) on Conversion Therapy in the UK, (signed by the NHS, Relate,

British Psychology Society, Pink Therapy, Mind, the Royal College of General Practitioners and 17 other leading medical, counselling and psychotherapy bodies) deems "conversion therapy" to be unacceptable, on the basis that this is "an umbrella term" ranging from any therapeutic approach to any individual viewpoint:

> ... that demonstrates an assumption that any sexual orientation or gender identity is inherently preferable to any other, and which attempts to bring about a change of sexual orientation or gender identity, or seeks to suppress an individual's expression of sexual orientation or gender identity on that basis.[72]

This means that the "practitioner" is, in the terms of the Memorandum:

> ... required to have adequate knowledge and understanding of gender and sexual diversity and to be free from any agenda that favours one gender identity or sexual orientation as preferable over other gender and sexual diversities. For this reason, it is essential for clinicians to acknowledge the broad spectrum of sexual orientations and gender identities and gender expressions.

There are serious questions to ask when it comes to statements about no sexual orientation or expression being preferable over another. Does this apply to paedophilia? Or to sex with animals or bestiality, varieties of sadomasochism and bondage, fetishisms or fixations on mutilation and so forth? Moreover, does 'conversion therapy' necessarily seek to "change or suppress" any sexual or gender identity on the basis of its inferiority to others?

4. What is allowed?

The UK Government's legislative proposals for bans can be simultaneously contradictory, reconciliatory, coercive and confusing. They describe how important it is "that a person experiencing gender dysphoria is able to openly explore what works for them without feeling pressured into any particular outcome". This purportedly recognises "that there are adults who seek counselling to help them live a life that they feel is more in line with their personal beliefs". The ban is said to "complement the existing clinical regulatory framework and not override the independence of clinicians to support those who may be questioning their LGBT status, in line with their professional obligations". This comes with the warning that supporting "a person who is questioning if they are LGBT" must not "start from the basis that being LGBT is a defect or deficiency" or "attempt to remedy or control this".[73]

Yet, if a person seeks to move away from anything with LGBT+ connections or connotations then, from their perspective it is something that they necessarily wish to "remedy or control". Should there not be "support" to help them move in the direction they want, rather than wasting their time being affirmed in something they don't want? Where has the promise gone that a "person experiencing gender dysphoria is able to openly explore what works for them without feeling pressured into any particular outcome"? Expressing a contradictory position, the "government's view is that this [the attempt to remedy an LGBT orientation] is wrong and ultimately constitutes conversion therapy". While therapy must ostensibly be "open, and explorative discussions focussed on helping a person to decide on their options in a supportive manner", the options are limited.

Because 'conversion therapy' can be extensively or broadly conceived, can it include expressing opinions that influence another's beliefs and/or actions? As seen in the Welsh example, bans on "all aspects of LGBTQ+ conversion therapy" extend to contesting "heteronormative and cisnormative assumptions". It is not clear whether this applies only to individuals' assumptions or means a more concerted sweep through education and communication to criminalise anything perceived as adverse on LGBTQ+ identity, orientation, lifestyle or perspectives.[74]

The often-quoted 2009 Report from the American Psychological Association (APA) or Task Force on Appropriate Therapeutic Responses to Sexual Orientation has played an influential role in barring change procedures. Psychologists unsympathetic to SOCE were appointed to this Task Force, with at least five of six members LGB identified. As a critic observed, while the "APA has every right to stack the deck however they wish on such matters ... they should at least publicly acknowledge that they represent a firmly and consistently left-of-center take on the science and politics of sexual orientation." Many other well-qualified, but more conservative, psychologists were nominated to serve on the Task Force, but all were rejected.[75]

A review of the literature on psychotherapy and sexual orientation available at the time, or journal articles in English from 1960 to 2007 (mainly before 1981), found that most had "serious methodological problems". Since few met basic standards for evaluating effects, there was no "kind of information needed for definitive answers to questions of safety and efficacy", with only self-reports of perceived benefits and harms from self-selected respondents. The Report could not "conclude how likely it is that harm will occur" or "draw a conclusion regarding whether recent forms of SOCE are or are not effective". Some change was recorded but, overall, nothing "significant ... that could be empirically validated ...". There were some studies of early "aversive forms of SOCE". These had high dropout rates, and it was "unclear what specific individual characteristics and diagnostic criteria" would later distinguish the recipients from any others who might perceive that they were harmed by SOCE. Moreover, it is not possible to determine to what extent any harm is a result of 'conversion therapy' rather than not accepting one's sexual orientation which might, in turn, be exacerbated by SOCE.

The APA did favour "affirmative therapeutic interventions" involving "the facilitation of clients' active coping, social support, and identity exploration ...", although "without imposing a specific sexual orientation identity outcome". This would "encourage APA to continue its advocacy for lesbian, gay, bisexual, and transgender individuals and families and to oppose prejudice against sexual minorities". It would also "encourage collaborative activities in pursuit of shared prosocial goals between psychologists and religious communities ... that are consistent with psychologists' professional and scientific roles".[76]

While the absence of definitive research results was underlined, the APA review has been taken as conclusive evidence that change cannot occur; attempts to facilitate this are therefore regarded as *ipso facto* harmful and it is assumed that support should concentrate on helping recipients accept being LGBT. The APA itself expressed concern that the practice of SOCE has "become mired in ideological disputes and competing political agendas" and, while it did not specifically recommend bans on professional SOCE practices, it is the hard-line interpretations which inspire contemporary prohibition moves, as seen in the work of the Government Equalities Office researchers.

The APA has been criticised for setting extraordinary standards of methodological rigour for this research area. Its Task Force concluded that future research on reorientation therapies should use methods that are prospective and longitudinal. Sampling methods must: allow for generalisation; use appropriate, objective, and high-quality measures of sexual orientation and identity; address pre-existing and co-occurring conditions, including mental health problems, other interventions, and life histories to test competing explanations for changes; and include measures capable of assessing harm. A contemporaneous examination of how existing studies of reparative therapy were conducted, had highlighted important omissions. Along with an absence of data for race, religious orientation, income, education and other demographic characteristics, the sample often lacked control groups and longitudinal follow-ups. Studies that failed even to report dropout rates effectively made drawing conclusions about treatment effectiveness extremely difficult, if not impossible. Along with emphasising the need for samples with precisely matched controls, the researchers emphasised how studies should not only monitor the long-term effects of interventions, but even the practitioner's ability to reverse any effects of reorientation therapies, so that the unsatisfied could be taken back to their former identities.[77]

Stanton L. Jones observes that "the entire mental health field" would:

> ... grind to a stop if the standards articulated for sexual orientation change were applied, for instance, to low self-esteem, depression, anxiety disorders, eating disorders, or personality disorders, or to any of the day-to-day stuff of mental health practice.[78]

The "virtually unparalleled, categorical view of change" taken by the APA would mean that any subsequent reappearance of depressive mood following treatment for depression should be viewed as an invalidation of genuine change, no matter how infrequently symptoms reoccur or diminished in intensity they are, if subsequently re-experienced.

After the 2009 APA report, there was a little noticed revision of APA claims that sexual orientation is 'not changeable', along with the opinion that attempts to change result in grave harm. In any event, opponents of change interventions have imposed "a much higher standard for methodological rigour when it comes to efficacy of change interventions than they do when addressing the potential for harm...".[79] This might also apply to the Coventry researchers for the Government Equality Office (GEO), discussed later.

A randomised controlled trial or 'gold standard' empirical investigation to assess changes to sexual orientation, behaviour or attraction attributable to particular therapies, with matched placebo groups, would certainly be very difficult for this subject (along with others in the psychiatric field). This would necessitate allocating a randomly selected group of people to different procedures or none, with controls for characteristics that might bias the findings and individuals followed over time. There are, however, recent investigations that have used various techniques to approximate to important aspects of this model arrangement.

Otherwise, studies in this field are often 'qualitative' or use retrospective self-reporting by self-selected or volunteer samples. These lend themselves easily to manipulation to achieve the desired results. Since those conducting studies may either be supporters of prohibitions who expect accounts of harms without change or, less likely, those hopeful of change without harms, results can endorse the researchers' standpoints. However, it is possible to carefully build up a knowledge base and establish possible (and always challengeable) connections through investigations with data checks and operative controls.

Opposition to SOCE from professional, commercial, and funding organisations, along with allegations of the 'damage' that accrues, all help to bring down the sledgehammer on investigation. Having established dominion over matters of sexual politics, groups like

Stonewall have come to exert control throughout media, together with academic, political and governing bodies in the UK. This disallows diversity in research, debate, or practice. It is an Anglophone-wide phenomenon. Activists are quick to move in on opponents, for instance, where in Toronto, Kenneth Zucker was sacked as head of the Child, Youth and Family Gender Identity Clinic, after accusations of conducting 'conversion therapy'.

In the UK, Bath Spa University barred James Caspian in 2017 from conducting research on the growing numbers of people de-transitioning because it feared this might cause offence and result in criticism of the university on social media. He was refused permission to continue with a bid for judicial review of the lawfulness of the university's decision to reject his proposal.[80] In this environment, few or none might want to conduct any research on so fraught a subject.

James Esses was dismissed as a volunteer counsellor with the charity Childline and asked to leave a five-year degree course after publicly raising concerns about youngsters confused about gender identity being automatically labelled transgender and fast-tracked into making life-altering decisions. This clashed with beliefs that children know their own minds about gender. He wanted "an open and honest debate about a hugely important topic – I'm not sure what is wrong with that…". It is telling how Esses was condemned for using the service to advance 'personal campaigns', since Childline and the NSPCC emphasised 'neutrality and non-alignment'. Yet, while these bodies purportedly offer a 'welcoming space for all', their response to gender dysphoric kids is described as resembling 'a roadmap towards transition.'[81] Is this the new 'neutrality' or orthodoxy?

Many professional and official bodies in Western societies have come to outlaw measures for those seeking help to avoid same-sex attraction/behaviour, with more underway. These are overwhelmingly signatories to Memoranda in which they commit to ending 'conversion' therapy within their professions.

The 2022 Memorandum of Understanding (MoU) on Conversion Therapy in the UK (sponsored by Pink Therapy and Stonewall) was, as mentioned, signed by 25 bodies from the Council for Psychotherapy to the NHS in England and Scotland.[82] As with the compilation of the APA guidelines, dissenting voices were excluded from participation in the development, while arguing that the public be "well informed" about the evidence for the harm and risks" of conversion therapy. Despite making this claim for "evidence", it cites no proper scientific investigation for assertions that "efforts to try to change or alter sexual orientation through psychological therapies are unethical and potentially [sic] harmful". Anyone endorsing or providing this therapy might now be barred from entry to training in psychotherapeutic practices, struck off, or denied collegiality within the professional and mental health fields or indemnity insurance. With threats of suspending or revoking the licences of medical professionals, school counsellors and psychologists, the message has become:

> Unless you want trouble, do not challenge the narrative
> of unquestioning 'affirmation' for every child who

claims to be trans – no matter the age, context, or lack of responsible medical oversight provided to the family.[83]

A psychiatrist is at risk for questioning whether gender reassignment is appropriate for a patient. This is backed up by claims that, since neither gender identity or sexual orientation can be regarded as an 'illness', they cannot be 'treated' or altered. In contrast, the "primary purpose" of professional bodies "is the protection of the public through a commitment to ending the practice [of] conversion therapy." [84]

From a different perspective, might dealing with prospective transgender patients involve efforts to resolve gender dysphoria by perhaps pausing intervention or reconciling patients to their own bodies? There is a significant contradiction here, when the MoU speaks of helping those across the UK (which has seen recent challenges). Removing the barriers has meant withdrawal from assessment of the capacity of youngsters to make decisions on transition, rendering those unhappy with their sexual orientation or gender identity unable to explore "therapeutic options to help them live more comfortably with it, reduce their distress and reach a greater degree of self-acceptance", when this does not apply to those seeking to leave their birth sex. As if to emphasise this 'one way only' dogma, a point is made that the advice is not "intended to stop medical professionals from prescribing hormone treatments and other medications to trans patients and people experiencing gender dysphoria". Procedures adopted by transgender clinics in recent years have come to make even any questioning of those seeking sex change exceedingly difficult, as 'watchful waiting' has been replaced by 'affirmation' of the patient's choice.

With the MoU suggesting no lower age limit on clients, this approach has been adopted by children's services assuming that children may give their formal and informed consent. The psychotherapy world has agreed that children who say they feel they are transgender should automatically go through the process if they "ask for it", with parents meant to approve a new identity and sex-change procedures if such is the child's wish. This is irrespective of whether it is appropriate treatment and the profound, lifelong impact of what are fundamentally experimental procedures resulting in irreversible physical changes. Therapists fear being labelled 'transphobic' if they question children's claims that they are really the other sex or investigate possible influences or underlying conditions.

Influential are care guidelines from the World Professional Association for Transgender Health [WPATH], based in Illinois in the US.[85] While considerately worded, the only way is affirmation. This talks of providing "family counseling and supportive psychotherapy to assist children and adolescents with exploring their gender identity, alleviating distress related to their gender dysphoria, and ameliorating any other psychosocial difficulties." As "part of the overall treatment plan", there should be "assessment of gender dysphoria and mental health, [and] the adolescent's eligibility for physical interventions ...". There is advice to "educate and advocate on behalf of gender dysphoric children, adolescents, and their families in their community (e.g., day care centers, schools, camps, other organizations)." Mental health "professionals should not dismiss or express a negative attitude towards nonconforming gender identities or indications of gender dysphoria" but "explore the nature and characteristics of a child's or adolescent's gender identity." With families reassuringly acknowledged to "play an important role in the psychological health and well-being of youth ... professionals should help families to have an accepting and nurturing response to the concerns of their gender dysphoric child or adolescent". Psychotherapy "should focus on reducing a child's or adolescent's distress related to the gender dysphoria and ... any other psychosocial difficulties" and support "youth pursuing sex reassignment", since it is unethical to withhold treatment for a child desperate to avoid developing into what they believe is their wrong sex.

This organisation advocates for children to be allowed to begin cross-sex hormones at 14, two years earlier than it previously recommended, and girls to have breast removal surgery from 15. WPATH has a global membership of about 3,000 people and is not an official health body, despite creating standards of care and being a major influence in the field of medical and psychotherapeutic practice. Although it includes professionals, it is part of a lobby for transgender advocates and those marketing transgender products. The increasing anxieties being expressed about its objectives run to allegations about fetishism relating to bodily modification or mutilation, particularly involving castration.[86]

The widescale adoption of affirmation has occurred as the traditional tiny population of those with gender identity disorder (GID) or gender dysphoria – often middle-aged men distressed by their biological sex – has been replaced by the waves of youngsters seeking sex change.[87] Amongst the former, GID has been estimated at around 1 in 10,000 for male-to-female and less than 1 in 25,000 for female-to-male. In the past, they would have needed a clinical diagnosis to embark on medical interventions to help them 'pass' as the opposite sex. Given the youth surge, gender identity disorder has become 'gender incongruence' to separate it from mental health connotations. This move reflects political or cultural, not scientific, developments.

Institutional compliance across the globe has meant that bans which make it illegal to question a conviction of being 'born in the wrong body' are accompanied by help for constructing a different body to reflect the 'real self' that is readily provided. However, there is no substantiated evidence that brain structures differ between gender incongruent and gender congruent people.

The German cabinet passed a law banning therapies meant to alter a young person's chosen 'gender identity' or sexual orientation from mid-2020. While therapy is still permitted for consenting adults, breaking the law could mean fines or imprisonment. The Health Minister opined that wherever 'reparative therapies' are performed, there is often severe physical and mental suffering. Therapies have become illegal in Malta, Switzerland,

Taiwan, Brazil, Ecuador and Germany. Valencia's provincial legislation prohibited therapy to turn a person's orientation away from homosexuality in 2018, with fines up to 120,000 euros for violators of the law.

In Australia, the Victoria Change and Suppression (Conversion) Practices Prohibition Act 2021 gives statutory recognition to what is described as "serious harm caused by change or suppression practices", both to the person subject to these and to the 'community' as a whole. Paediatrician Felicity Nelson celebrates Australian "clinical guidelines which state that 'withholding of gender-affirming treatment is not considered a neutral option' as it may exacerbate distress, depression, anxiety or suicidality". With "transgender and queer youth" described as "already at incredibly high risk … to deny treatment due to an ideological war is inexcusable".[88] In Queensland and Capital Territory, parents who do not cooperate with the decision of their 'trans child' for sex-change may face criminal proceedings and even prison, along with doctors or counsellors who fail to offer affirmative support. They should not object to puberty-blockers, opposite-sex hormones, and possible surgical procedures to amputate and mutilate organs and body parts.

Similarly, for New Zealand, it could be a criminal offence for family members to "attempt to change or suppress the sexual orientation, gender identity or expression of children" or deploy 'practices' that discourage anyone from expressing or realising their 'gender identity', such as trying to stop a youngster taking puberty blockers. Complaints can also be made to the Human Rights Commission and the Human Rights Review Tribunal. The Ministry of Justice has it that while "criminal offences and penalties and the civil redress process in themselves may not bring about a complete end to conversion practices ... they would send a strong message that such practices are not tolerated...".[89]

Canada Bill C-4 passed without dissent. This targets any practice, treatment or service designed to "change a person's sexual orientation to heterosexual, or gender expression to cisgender or a person's gender expression to conform to the sex assigned to them at birth", or to repress or reduce non-heterosexual attraction or sexual behaviour. Depending on interpretations, this potentially outlaws prayer and counselling between pastors and congregants, and conversations between parents and children. Canada's Minister of Justice explained that it was designed to "discourage and denounce harmful practices and treatments that are based on myths and stereotypes about LGBTQ2 people", including how "the sexual orientation, gender identity or gender expression of LGBTQ2 people are undesirable conditions that can or should be changed". With prospects of jail for anyone "disrespectful" enough to question the prohibition, this may include parents if they continue to recognize their child's biological sex by, for example, using the birth name, or refusing to let a son wear a dress and take puberty blockers.[90]

The Canadian state has fully taken on the tenets of transgenderism and gender fluidity, where people must accept that individuals can be assigned the 'wrong sex' at birth, while those who disagree should not raise this in discussion, even with children. Promises might have been made that "new offences would not criminalise private conversations … where teachers, school counsellors, pastoral counsellors, faith leaders, doctors, mental health professionals, friends or family members provide support to persons struggling with their sexual orientation, sexual feelings, or gender identity". However, like suggestions for UK legislation, the inference is that this "support" is not for heterosexuality or natal sex. Since discussions that take place during a gender transition must not assume "that a particular … gender identity or gender expression is to be preferred over another", this is unlikely to cover a gender-confused person being told that that they would be better off reflecting their biological sex and staying as their male or female self.[91] After a lengthy contest, one father was jailed for insisting on referring to his 'daughter' with female pronouns. She was given her preferred sex at a very transgender-affirming school and received testosterone injections at 12 years of age.[92]

While conversion or change therapy is fully or partially outlawed in about 20 US states, there has been some anxiety that all-age bans could contravene the old ethical principle of client autonomy. In July 2018, Maine's Governor, Paul LePage, perceptively vetoed legislation that would have banned therapists from helping minors with unwanted same-sex attraction or gender confusion. State law already prohibited practices that amount to physical or mental abuse, and evidence had not been produced that "conversion" therapy was being practised.

Much evidence indicates how UK proposals to make it "illegal not to affirm the claims of 'trans children'" will create a parental and pedagogic nightmare.[93] Criminalisation might befall anything other than immediate acceptance and encouragement of a child's new sexual or gender identity, regardless of age. There are assurances that anyone can be helped to "explore or come to terms with their identity in a non-judgmental and non-directive way". Is this a trap, which could be triggered when someone is not approving a new identity or makes an inadmissible judgment or comment?[94]

By early 2022, there was growing realisation that the proposed 'conversion therapy' ban was more than a move simply to addressing 'coercive and abhorrent' treatment, or a symbolic gesture to reassure identity groups. Suddenly, Downing Street announced that the Prime Minister had decided against making it illegal to 'change or suppress' a person's sexuality or gender identity. Since a ban was being recognised as applying to counselling, concerns were rising about the profound consequences for those working with youngsters who had gender dysphoria. There was also lately awareness of the existing laws against 'coercive and abhorrent' behaviours, including the Criminal Justice Act, Offences Against the Person Act and Domestic Abuse Act. Nikki da Costa, the former director of legislative affairs at No 10, had spoken of creating a situation where doctors, therapists and parents would be deterred from investigating what else may be going on with a child's mental health for fear that they will be accused of trying to change the child's gender identity or sexual orientation.

As the Prime Minister's official spokeswoman said: "Having explored this sensitive issue in great depth the government has decided to proceed by reviewing how existing law can be deployed more effectively to prevent this in the quickest way possible and explore the use of other non-legislative measures."

There was an immediate backlash from LGBT campaign groups and some Parliamentarians. Downing Street advisers warned that the 'LGBT sector' would read this as a signal the government was uninterested in their issues. Jayne Ozanne was "livid" with Mr Johnson and his "betrayal" of the LGBT+ community – arguing that it would put lives at risk. The "decision will leave countless LGBT+ people completely undefended from degrading abuse … and will embolden perpetrators to continue their horrific acts with impunity". Labour said the "outrageous decision" showed that the Prime Minister could not be taken at his word on LGBT+ rights. Liberal Democrat equalities spokesperson, Vera Hobhouse MP, added that Tories were "giving the green light to a form of torture in the UK. This is an utter betrayal of the LGBT+ community."[95]

In the evening of the same day, Johnson did another U-turn and, backtracking a second time, reinstated the commitment to ban 'conversion therapy', but with gender dysphoria excluded from the legislation. Alicia Kearns MP was pleased by Johnson's reversal but criticised the exclusion of trans people, as Ozanne's hope that law would "protect … particularly trans people who are the most at risk" was dashed.[96] "Why should quacks and charlatans be allowed to continue to cause life-long harm to them?", Kearns posted on Twitter, after attributing her support for a ban to what she had seen depicted in fictional media drama.

By Spring 2022, Johnson's method of policy by throwaway soundbites left the government's position over the 'conversion therapy' ban in confusion. Summing it all up, and whether for or against "stopping the nonsense of 'conversion'", according to Matthew Parris:

> ... what is indefensible is for a prime minister to scuttle from one opinion to the other at the first sound of gunfire. Any presumption that he believed in the policy he first adopted is shattered. We must assume somebody had advised him to do a pro-gay thing and now somebody else has advised him that this will alienate some anti-gay people.[97]

There might be more controversy in store as Labour aims to amend forthcoming legislation to include transgender rights, given how the Government has appeared to have side-lined a previous Tory administration's proposals for radical reform of gender change legislation.

Chapter Two

WORLDS OF FIXED AND FLUID

1. Contrasting perspectives

The concept of gender and sexual identities as integral to personhood is largely a given in public discourse. Tied to recognition and rights, these categories of identity possess a recognised, established status as inviolate, ring-fenced identities that warrant protection from any assault on their authenticity. Being transgender has come to represent a similar fixed intrinsic state of being, or an all-encompassing essence of personhood, or 'born that way' which may be at odds with the sex that is now construed by the LGBT 'community' and its supporters in politics and the media as arbitrarily 'assigned' at birth.

When dissent is equated to rejecting people because of what they are, then, as understood by activists, support is best ensured by claiming that something is innate, or an irrevocable core of being. The argument goes that, at the very least, a person should not be held responsible for characteristics over which they have no choice or control and that they should be defended if they feel that they are being intimidated, bullied or discriminated against for what they did not ask to be. A lifelong, inherent identity commands affirmation, not denial.

While the affirmative perspective accepts that a person can become uncomfortable with heterosexuality and move to embrace homosexuality, the alternative of moving to heterosexuality is not equivalent, let alone better, and anyone is said to be under a misconception if they think otherwise. As someone observed, the "needs of the collective outrank the personal rights of the individual to decide their sexual orientation".[98]

There is a question here which has not been resolved: "If gays have achieved the same rights as everyone else, should they be subjected to the same standards as everyone else? Or is there built into gay equality some kind of opt-out? Should a gay couple be expected to be monogamous just as heterosexual couples are expected to be?" There is uncertainty whether "most gays want to be completely equal" or maybe "precisely equal but with a little gay bonus".[99] They are already a 'protected category' in law, which confers special consideration. This protection might appear to underpin the essentialist viewpoint – where a person's sexual orientation or gender identity is irremovably ingrained, absolute and unchangeable, finalised and fixed, notwithstanding that this might limit choice.

In juxtaposition, fluidity and choice are opportunistic and experimental. The goals of sections of the LGBT 'community' go beyond acceptance, and encompass a radical flight from all sexual categorisation. These challenge any views that sex or sexual behaviours constitute the truth of the human individual. Instead, it is those unburdened by exclusive sexual attributions or attachments who represent a universal potential for the realisation of all sexual pleasures and embodiments throughout society and life. The true radical, or 'queer' as it used to be, might even construe specific ring-fenced identities as imposing new forms of control. Equality might suggest living like respectable straight people, with monogamous marriages, homes and children, or like "everybody else, other than in one single characteristic". This is what those with a revolutionary 'queer' outlook have sought to overthrow.

As Peter Tatchell put it:

> Apart from die-hard homophobes, who could possibly disagree with equality? I can! Call me ungrateful and pushy, but I don't like the way the lesbian and gay community has dumbed-down its aspirations to the flawed goal of equal rights. Whatever happened to the lofty ideals of gay liberation and sexual freedom? During the 1990s, there was a dramatic shift in the homosexual zeitgeist – from defining our needs on our terms, to meekly falling in with the prevailing heterosexual consensus. The dominant gay agenda is now equal rights and law reform, rather than gay emancipation and the transformation of society.

For Tatchell, the "price" of equality is "parity on straight terms, within a pre-existing framework of values, laws and institutions ... devised by and for the heterosexual majority" and requiring "conformity to their rules". This is a recipe for "incorporation, not liberation" or "a policy of social assimilation" which is not about "respecting difference, but obliterating it". He attributes homosexuals' difficulties not just to homophobia, but "the more general eroto-phobic and sex-negative nature of contemporary culture (which also harms heterosexuals)" seen in censorship of sexual imagery, inadequate sex education, and the criminalisation of sex workers and consensual sadomasochistic relationships. The "'good gays' are rewarded" while "all the sex-repressive social structures, institutions and value systems remain intact …". [100]

The complaint might have been premature. It has not taken long for "terms such as straight, gay and bisexual" to perhaps become an outdated "'binary' view of sexuality." Now, well into the 21st century, this is described as "fast becoming the equivalent of walking around in plus-fours, peering at human desire through a monocle". People, particularly in their teens and twenties, are "declaring themselves 'pansexual', 'genderfluid' and 'genderqueer', and won't be confined to the old folks' dreary, black-and-white view of attraction or gender". [101] Similarly, some do not want to climb from one gender into another, but they prefer being third-way 'non-binary and genderqueer', switching day-by-day, or remaining in a genderless space between the two.

As youngsters are enticed with buffets of experiences that they might like to try, a 'resource' available from the BBC for children aged nine to twelve, *Understanding Sexual and Gender Identities*, claimed that there are over 100 'gender identities'. [102] In 2019, the US Trevor Project (purporting to be the world's largest suicide prevention and crisis intervention organisation for LGBTQ youth) added "exposure to conversion therapy" to "challenges that LGBTQ youth across the country face every day…". [103] The project spoke of being "particularly proud that it is inclusive of youth of more than 100 sexual orientations and more than 100 gender identities from all 50 states across the country". Sexual orientations range from 'heteroflexible' to 'panromantic asexual' [sic] to 'greyromantic demisexual' to 'queer demisexual' to 'biromantic' to 'sexually fluid abrosexual'. Gender identities range from 'gender-fluid non-binary' to 'boyflux' to 'androgyn' to 'gender apathetic'.

Outright 'liberation' allies itself with other movements aimed at overturning the society into which others seek acceptance. Along with the disruptive antics and marches in the streets with the demonstrators in BDSM fetish gear, or 'exhibitionism for activism', the new century's wave of racial and transgender aspirations has re-fuelled abiding aspirations for dissolving sexual membership, smashing capitalism and abolishing the family. (This is ironic when leading businesses routinely fund and publicise powerful LGBT organisations.) A big issue for the radical is "whether being gay means that you are attracted to members of your own sex, or whether it means that you are part of a grand political project".[104]

Variable choice as an alternative to fixed propensities has its own problems. It is questionable whether, like many other human dispositions, matters of sexual desire, attraction and behaviour – or gender identification – result from 'choice' in terms of discrete, conscious, deliberate decisions or rational calculations. There may be instances, but behaviour patterns are usually owed to many influences or complex amalgams of habits, experience, pressures, opportunities, incentives, affiliations, fantasies and genetics – affecting how individuals adopt and abandon different stances over life, in both the short and long term.[105]

Inconsistent though it is, and however sexual orientation or sexual propensities may be acquired, in the discourse about 'conversion therapy', fixed and fluid converge on a one-way street. As it has come to be, heterosexuality is perceived as certainly not better or even equal to having a gay identity. Any movement in the direction of heterosexuality might be threatening, or challenging to the LGBTQ immutability perspective, just as it might also demean representatives of future inclusivity. As Douglas Murray observes, when:

> ... people come out as gay they are celebrated for having arrived at their natural end-point ... there is no problem with them being what they are: they have arrived at the place that is natural and right for them. But the oddity of this position is that anybody who is gay and subsequently decides they are straight will be the subject not just of a degree of ostracism and suspicion, but widespread doubt that they are being honest about their true selves. A straight who becomes gay has settled. A gay who has become straight has rendered himself an object of permanent suspicion.

> For many gay men and women the idea that sexuality is fluid and that what goes one way may go another (what goes up must come down) is an attack on their person. ... since the phase 'It's only a phase' is offensive for some people, the idea that it might actually be true for some people is unsayable.[106]

Even as a "younger generation is exploring sexual 'fluidity'" the "activists keep assuming that being gay (and trans) is a totally fixed identity which must always and only be affirmed, there is no flow the other way."[107] As activists' hope to expand LGBTQI+ membership, the encouragement of greater fluidity for all sits somewhat incongruously with a view of the solidity of sexual and gender identities.

It is now accepted that help to change in the direction of heterosexuality, of any description or any degree, must not be available to anybody, whatever their wishes. This extends to transgender people wanting to transition back to their biological sex. Deirdre McCloskey (who is trans) insists that it is mistaken to:

> ... believe that a sound reason to oppose gender change in say, children, is the alleged 'accounts of detransitioners'. The overwhelming bulk of transitioners, male-female or female-male ..., are happy with their decision, whether they did it as children or as adults. 'Ecstatic' is how I would describe it. I did it at age 53 in 1995...

But, for her:

> TERFs [Trans Exclusionary Radical Feminists] fiercely oppose free choices by others, choices that do no harm to any of them ... they tell each other fairy tales about 'men' sneaking around female public conveniences and about trans people 'regretting' their transitions. The dogma is a set of hateful prejudices.[108]

To serve this end, 'conversion therapy' is the dragon to slay. Provocateur Milo Yiannopoulos might be throwing a grenade into the 'identity is for life' consensus, as he declared himself 'ex-gay', 'sodomy free' and Christian in early 2021. He wanted to rehabilitate 'conversion therapy'; he likened homosexuality to 'addiction'; he called transsexuals 'demonic', and he questioned how anyone could be "wholly at home in the gay lifestyle". He was flaunting this in public to "drive liberals crazy to see a handsome, charismatic, intelligent gay man riotously celebrating conservative principles".[109]

Was this sincere or a publicity stunt? If he was only acting, it might affirm the permanency perspective. Otherwise, by exposing the fixed verses fluid quandary, how are political commentators to behave if they "risk sounding bigoted if they state how overjoyed they are that Milo has abandoned their favourite victimhood category, while at the same time expressing fury over anyone changing their mind about a sexual preference?"[110]

In relation to the prospects of harm for the patient or victim from change procedures, important to lobby groups is the devaluation and denial of a person's true and immutable sexual identity or gender. Could this mean that ex-gay or ex-trans testimonies, like that from Milo Yiannopoulos, be treated as offences when aired at public gatherings, including online? Are ex-gay and ex-trans people shameful for their life choices?

Chapter Three

WHAT TO FORBID?

1. What is happening?

Before measures to ban something proceed, it might help to know how many cases or victims are out there and what they actually experience. Generating a proper estimate of the prevalence of 'conversion therapy' requires accurate information. As such, there is no representative or robust data on the number of LGBT people who have received conversion therapy in the UK, or who is most likely to undergo, be offered, or want this.

More or less the only study, the National LGBT Survey 2017 found that, of the 108,000 people who responded, 2% had previously undergone 'conversion therapy' to leave being LGBT, and a further 5% had been offered this or 'reparative therapy'. These figures were higher for trans respondents (9% of trans men had been offered it and 4% had undergone it). This is a volunteer, self-reporting sample recruited at LGBT pride events, and through social and national media coverage. It is not representative of LGBT people in the UK or those who have sought or received change therapy and therefore does not cover results or how long ago any took place. Excluded from the onset would have been those who no longer identified as gay or lesbian or did not generally associate with a 'gay community'.

The survey "did not provide a definition of conversion therapy" or of "techniques intended to change someone's sexual orientation or gender identity", except to state that these "can range from pseudo-psychological treatments to spiritual counselling. In extreme cases, they may also include surgical and hormonal, or so called 'corrective' rape." The respondents may have different experiences compared with people who did not wish to disclose their LGBT status, or no longer identified as such. To correct for this potential sample bias, statistical manoeuvring produced figures of 2.9% for respondents who received, and 5% who were offered, conversion therapy.[111] Figures from the US, for exposure to psychological attempts to change a person's gender identity from transgender to 'cisgender' were 13.5% over lifetime for a sample of 27,716 transgender people and 5% for transgender adults between 2010 and 2015.[112] For 51% of those who received 'conversion' or 'reparative therapy' in the UK sample, this was from faith bodies, followed by healthcare professionals (19%). Otherwise, family members or other organisations or acquaintances were involved. Bisexual respondents were the least likely to have received or been offered any (5%), lower than for asexual respondents (10%). Transgender respondents were more likely to have undergone or been offered 'conversion therapy' (13%) than natal-sex respondents (7%), although this did not distinguish those who underwent therapy to change their sexual orientation from any who wished to change their gender identity. The latter were less likely to have undergone conversion therapy by faith bodies (45%) than other respondents (53%).

Not deterred by how "the exact prevalence of conversion therapy is challenging to establish", it is nonetheless "the view of the government that one incident of conversion therapy is too many".[113] If this is referring to some torture or coercive procedure then, again, there are laws to deal with it. If this is more than hyperbole, does one incident justify an expensive, intrusive, multi-faceted intervention when, not least, there are many other contenders for resources? Should a particular section of the population be granted such importance?

Along with questions about who has sought or received 'conversion therapy' is how many health professionals are providing this? The Government Equalities Office has not held such information.

A UK-based survey of a random sample of members of four leading UK psychotherapy and psychiatric organisations back in 2009 found that only 4% of therapists reported that they would attempt to change a client's sexual orientation when asked.[114] A higher proportion (17%) reported having assisted at least one client to reduce or change homosexual feelings. The 222 professionals who had helped clients with these issues answered the question: "Given the extent of knowledge about homosexuality and treatments available to change or redirect homosexual or lesbian feelings, are there any circumstances where people should have the opportunity to reduce or redirect their homosexual or lesbian feelings?" One hundred and fifty-nine (72%) agreed and 28 (13%) disagreed with the statement, while 35 (15%) gave no answer. The reasons for seeking help were summarised as confusion about sexual orientation (57%), social pressures including from families (14%), mental health difficulties (11%), religious beliefs (7%), gender confusion (4%), legal pressures (4%), heterosexual relationship difficulties (2%), and being victims of abusive relationships (2%).

The professionals involved considered that a client/patient's distress about their homosexuality was justification for intervention, citing religious, cultural and moral values as likely causes for internal conflict. For one therapist: "where someone had a strong faith, then working to help the person accept their feelings but manage them appropriately may be the best approach…". For another: "In many societies/cultures, expression of sexuality out [of kilter] with cultural norms can cause huge distress. Given the balance between biological and developmental determinants of sexuality, it is valid for an individual to value his cultural norms and to try and reduce the distress caused by transgressing these." There are "those within marriages that wish to continue with that relationship rather than break up". Another cites how the "homosexual man I helped to become heterosexual came from a working class background where it was completely unacceptable to deviate from the norm. It was extremely important to him to be accepted by that community."

The wishes of the client/patient were "mentioned by all groups of practitioners, with self-determination being seen as an issue that might override a degree of professional unease …". Here, people "should have the choice to explore change while at the same time the therapist can hold to their ethical stance." If, "after extensive, good therapy, they were still adamant they wanted to change … this was their decision though I would hope they would come to terms with themselves on the journey." Certainly: "people should have the opportunity to consider their sexuality and if they want to reduce or redirect any aspect of it, they should be helped to do so", since psychiatrists had "a responsibility to assist our patients with self-determination". After all, many who go for change procedures may, in some senses, have already rejected an LGB identity, practices or attractions.

Children and young adults were described as "more likely to be confused … and to jump to conclusions (correct or otherwise) if unable to talk through their concerns". Some "professionals considered that a history of sexual abuse had possibly had an impact on sexual preference and for this reason clients wished to reduce or redirect their same sex attraction." There may be a "need both to explore people's sexuality rather than to change it" where it was "up to the person themselves to decide in which direction to go. I am just the sounding board for them to make their own decisions", since helping "to clarify the situation is important".

Seemingly disappointed at these practitioners' responses, the researchers concluded that, "Given lack of evidence for the efficacy of such treatments, this is likely to be unwise or even harmful." But it was not clear why similar standards are not applied elsewhere. Therapy in this context is often viewed as a rigid, mono-enterprise which is out to 'convert' one sexual orientation into another. The reality may be far from attempts to change an individual from being gay to being straight, and more an exploration of the history of unwanted feelings or predilections, along with a discussion as to if and how these may be managed or subject to change.

In reality, outcomes in counselling or therapy are seldom clear-cut or predictable; nor are all practitioners equally skilled. Such considerations apply to many problems for which people seek help. There need be no primary purpose for psychiatric practice in terms of complete change – in any direction. There need be no assumption, as might be suggested by the Memorandum of Understanding, that a particular sexual orientation is inherently preferable or superior to another. Usually, change is on a continuum. Moreover, accepting that change is possible does not mean that everyone can change or that "changes are categorical, resulting in uncomplicated, dichotomous and unequivocal reversal of sexual orientation from completely homosexual to completely heterosexual".[115]

Something which also gets overlooked here is how "any discussion of alleged harms simply must be placed in the broader context of psychotherapy outcomes in general".[116] Reviews of results for specific disorders and treatments show that, while "psychotherapy has proven to be highly effective", not all clients report or show benefits. In turn, research offers "substantial ... evidence that psychotherapy can and does harm a portion of those it is intended to help." These include "the relatively consistent portion of adults (5% to 10%) and a shockingly high proportion of children (14% to 24%) who deteriorate while participating in treatment". Regardless of the client's ostensible problems and stated goals, any psychotherapy can result in no or poor outcomes.[117]

The castigation of 'change therapy' also happens in conjunction with the toleration of multiple 'alternative' therapies like homeopathy, crystal healing and so forth. These and 'new age' healing or holistic treatment are patient 'choices', even if these may stop sick people receiving effective treatments that could save their health or even their lives. Some are endorsed and even promoted in the UK's National Health Service. A significant example might be 'natural' childbirth. This practice contributed to the deaths of many mothers and babies, as revealed by recent investigations into mortality and injury levels in some NHS trusts.

Many people with all manner of health or other problems recover or improve irrespective of whether the proffered remedy they might have used contributed. This enables many dubious 'cures' for various ills to claim success. This must always be borne in mind; the patient(s) may have changed anyway, therapy or no therapy. Again, people seeking cures are adults, who *want* a solution, which is important to the chances of success.

Ironically, "those with a taste for combining bad metaphysics and bad psychology can engage in past life regression therapy. In New York City, a therapist can tell a man with gender dysphoria that he is a reincarnation of Napoleon, but not that he is a man."[118] If an adult does not like their sexuality, and freely chooses even some half-baked change procedure to alter this, must they not have the right and freedom to do so?

The assumption that homosexuality is a "mental disease" is long gone. People may want to reduce or lose all manner of behaviours, habits and practices, from pornography addictions, to nervous reactions to any experiences or incidents. Dissatisfaction is not disorder or 'mental disease'. Across the world, juries are out on whether many other dispositions once labelled in terms of mental aberrations are really pathologies. There are no easy answers or instant cures for many unwanted predilections or tendencies. Some people manage to walk away when they are determined to do so, or after a particular experience. There may be positive changes or benefits from many therapies, irrespective or independently of modifications to the problem that was the initial reason for seeking help.

People can certainly be persuaded or pressurised to undergo procedures for various habits or propensities, and some measures could lie outside professional regulation. The Coventry University researchers for the Government Equalities Office report speak of "external pressure or coercion by family members or people from one's faith", with some feeling their 'choices' were "shaped by powerful influences in their social environment and under guidance from authority figures" even if "they underwent conversion therapy voluntarily".[119]

As social beings, people conform to a kaleidoscope of norms and, perhaps depending on the importance attached by others, there may be pressure of varying degrees to enforce compliance. Many may quietly or rudely not conform to expectations. There will be aspects of religious tenets that church attendees do not subscribe to, and this applies to membership of many groups or organisations. Depending on circumstances, levels of disagreement, commitment and available options, people can walk away.

Other reasons given for seeking conversion therapy include: "a desire to belong and feel part of a community", perhaps with suggestions from relatives and friends. Individuals may personally consider their homosexual or bisexual inclinations and behaviour to be incompatible with their religious faith and be unable to integrate the two identities. They may be dissatisfied or discomforted by same-sex experiences, which they find incompatible with their interests and personality, or what they want as a 'normal' life.

If someone relates their sexuality to how, for example, they were earlier recruited into gay life and now wish to leave, should they be forbidden to discuss this with a professional? Should a therapist be struck off for working with anyone when the possibility is that their sexuality may be far from solidly fixed? To remain faithful, a bisexual married man may wish to keep his same-sex desires in check. So, is he only allowed to consolidate these desires and leave his family? Someone may want a conventional family with a mother, father and children; should they be denied possible help?

The GEO's Coventry researchers are seemingly averse to recognising that someone may not want a 'homosexual lifestyle'. The gay scene might not be to everyone's taste; some could have issues with promiscuity, drugs, violence, or the risks from sexually transmitted diseases. There may be negative associations with same-sex sexuality or a history of unwanted or abusive sexual experiences. Shouldn't people be allowed to discuss these things if they wish, instead of being denied freedom to obtain help to more shape their predispositions in accord with what they see as a more authentic persona?[120] Are these just 'victims' of society in some shape or form, or perfectly capable of making a voluntary request in accordance with their values and needs?

Where a therapist, counsellor or even a priest cannot talk to someone who seeks their advice without threat of prosecution, is leaving them without help or support not a form of abuse?

2. Psychiatric practice?

Questions were put to Dr Christopher Rosik, a practising psychologist and director of research, at Link Care Center in Fresno, California, asking him to explain and defend what they do. He spoke of therapists who "typically utilize a number of mainstream interventions that address relevant emotional and cognitive processes as well as certain relational dynamics". They often "are not focusing on same-sex attractions at all, but rather on the broader issues of identity ... in an attempt to resolve various factors that may contribute to the patient's difficulties".

> While many of these therapists operate from a psycho-dynamic and developmental perspective, they often incorporate insights from the cognitive, interpersonal, narrative, and psychodrama traditions as well ... For those patients who prioritize their traditional religious and/or cultural values above acting upon their same-sex attractions, chastity/celibacy, behavioral manage-

ment, and the modification of same-sex attractions and behaviors are all valid options that should be embraced by their faith communities.

Rosik emphasises that, while fluidity is not uncommon, there is also the:

> … possibility [that] many non-heterosexual male activists who fight against a client's right to pursue professional care for unwanted same-sex attractions are men who have not experienced change and who assume that this is the case for all non-heterosexuals. Therefore, they may erroneously assume that all claims of change must either be lies or self-deception.

He also sees some counsellors wandering "too far from what current science says (or does not say) about sexual orientation". This results in "overselling the likelihood and degree of change, not sufficiently exploring the role of outside pressure on the client's motivation to pursue change, offering reductionist explanations for homosexuality" and so forth.

Also described is how psychotherapy patients "drop out of therapy with some regularity" and this, in itself, is:

> … not a clear indicator of harm. Some may drop out because of dissatisfaction, but others may drop out because they are doing better and no longer feel a need to continue in therapy. Some patients do decide to adopt a gay identity, and that is their right. As a psychologist, I am obligated to honor that decision as well.

Emphasised is how "questionable practices are kept to a minimum by accountability to a professional code of ethical conduct, including full informed consent and careful assessment of client motivation." For any adolescent patients, there is little or no attention to change, with the "main focus [on] ... working with the parents and encouraging them to love their child and keep the lines of communication open ..."[121]

In general, conversion or change therapy largely involves 'talking therapies' and spiritual interventions. There can be a mishmash of derivative psychoanalytic theories and procedures, including 'regression therapy', which might reflect popular notions of psychotherapy. This may probe for 'causes' of unwanted sexual orientation or gender identity in childhood 'traumas', family relationships (like a distant relationship with a parent) and 'unmet needs' or 'stored anger'. This goes along with the acting out of past events to 'release' repressed emotions to help 'heal' the 'brokenness'.

More practical and empirically based interventions may involve behaviour modifications or advice about 'healthy relationships'. Again, therapy (talking and listening) is unlikely to operate with a promise of changing a client's sexuality, home in on an endpoint or predetermine the outcome. Even if the issues that people bring to counselling include seeking help and support for leaving a lifestyle they reject, the emphasis may be more on relationships than behaviour, or *vice versa*. There may be moves to reframe desires, redirect thoughts, model new behaviours, avoid instigators and so forth in processes sometimes akin to dealing with addictions or compulsive behaviours. As taking such a course might seem for some to liken "feelings of same-sex attraction or being transgender to ... addiction", this could qualify for what government sees as making an unacceptable equation with defects or deficiencies. After all, the UK Government takes the view that: as any "attempt to remedy or control this ... would amount to conversion therapy ... our approach will target such practices".[122]

There is very limited evidence regarding the methods used to change gender identity compared with sexuality. A systematic review found only four relevant studies, but therapeutic psychiatric approaches were similar, with psychoanalytic and behavioural techniques. [123]

Restrictions and bans on 'conversion' or 'change' procedures are likely to constrain available assistance along with choice – in accordance with campaigners' aims; this is the remit. If, perfectly sanely, someone wishes to follow their own personal convictions regarding how they want to live out their sexuality and relationships, it will be difficult for them to find support as the quality and quantity of the help available falls. It will become uncertain if and where any is obtainable and who the practitioners might be. There could be qualified therapists operating under the radar. Otherwise, trained counsellors or psychotherapists might be thin on the ground. Alternatives may be 'pastoral' guides or volunteers from charities, church groups or other medical or pseudo specialities. As laws are introduced to ban therapies, they will restrict practices and publicity. Providers may rebrand and adapt their public messages.[124] These may claim to be treating 'trauma' or addiction, or offering 'reintegration' even if, along the way, a side-effect might be changes to sexuality or gender identity.

Those who wish to eradicate any 'change' or 'conversion' provisions may be pleased to see how their cause is vindicated by a lack of options, along with the possible disappointment or distress for those who have accessed what may then be left in the shape of ill-informed and poorly managed procedures. A low standard of therapeutic content comes across in some available accounts of change procedures.

If there is a demand for services, should a focus not be on researching and possibly developing properly authenticated practices, rather than clamping down to appease strident factions? This means a proper investigation of who seeks change and in what form or dimension, together with appraisal of outcomes for different interventions or therapy variants, along with an analysis of the results for patients with various attributes and objectives.

Perhaps from an unexpected direction comes dissenter Dominic Davies, the CEO of Pink Therapy. He spoke at the Department of Health Round Table on *Training and Policy relating to Conversion Therapy* in 2014 about how "understanding what is different about working with gender or sexual minorities is either absent or patchy in most British therapy training courses …". As sexuality was fluid for many, there was great variation in those seeking change and a "big stick or forbidding conversion therapy is not helpful. You have a duty of care to your members to support them to know how best to effectively respond to genuine distress and requests for 'cure'." Prohibitions might get imposed with theological 'conversions' in mind, but most patients may not be overtly religiously motivated and, anyway, forbidding something doesn't make it go away. In his experience:

> ... sexuality can be quite plastic for many people and there are plenty of examples of situational homosexuality amongst heterosexuals in single sex environments and sexual fluidity over a lifespan for many LGB and T people ...

To Davies, the correct, non-discriminatory position was not to be 'hetero-centred', or focused on immutable identities, but more pick and mix. The answer for bisexuals seeking counselling may not be simply to "pick one identity and either be heterosexual or gay". With research showing that between 50-80% of gay male couples were not sexually exclusive, dealing with their relationship problems may mean help with managing open relationships as much as maintaining sexual fidelity.[125] For ambivalent or indecisive cases, psychotherapy might more fruitfully focus on increasing active coping rather than pursuing orientation change.[126]

3. Self-help?

Accusations of 'conversion therapy' are speeded on by campaigns of aggressive trolling, with attempts to de-platform anyone who says change is possible; these involve closing accounts and placing bans on psychiatric help or counselling, which include informal measures.

In 2019, an app that advised people on 'recovery from same-sex attraction' was removed from Google's Play store after one leading US LGBTQ charity suspended the tech company from its gay and transgender rights ranking over the software. This Human Rights Campaign (HRC) also removed the search giant from its annual Corporate Equality Index, which ranks US companies on the benefits they offer LGBTQ staff. The app was "life-threatening to LGBTQ youth and also clearly violates the company's own standards", an HRC spokesperson told *Dailymail.com*. (Since 2017, Google had donated $1.5m to the LGBT Center of New York's Stonewall Forever project, which records gay and transgender history online and would continue making similar donations.)[127]

Openly gay State Senator Brad Hoylman joined in the calls to take down the app after signing into law a prohibition on 'conversion therapy' in New York. Finding Google's position "mind-boggling [sic] and personally offensive" he saw "no place for homophobia, on or off-line in our society". The app "is degrading LGBTQ people, which can be the basis of hatred towards this community". In consultation with 'outside advocacy groups', Google said that it had acquired a "thorough understanding of the app and its relation to conversion therapy".

Amazon, Apple and Microsoft stores removed material designed by the Christian group *Living Hope Ministries,* which aims to help people 'struggling with same gender attraction'. Facebook deleted the page of Christian ministry *Core Issues Trust* (CIT), which aims to help people who voluntarily seek to change their sexual attraction and supports former LGBTs. Across services, CIT staff were blocked from posting and unable to stop trolls. Targeted through a social media campaign, CIT was dropped by multiple service providers, such as Mailchimp and PayPal, which restricts the ability of supporters to make donations. Barclays

Bank closed its accounts, videos were taken down and Instagram content removed. At the command of *Pink News*, *Vue* Cinemas cancelled a showing of *Voices of the Silenced*, a documentary from ex-gay Christian, Mike Davidson. It did pay a fee for breach of contract, while insisting that the film went against its 'values'. The film has testimonies from ex-gays – some with faces blacked out and others not.

Davidson had appeared as a guest in 2017 on ITV's *Good Morning Britain* to discuss the counselling his group offered to people who might wish to move away from homosexuality or towards heterosexuality. On the programme he said that he regarded homosexuality as a learnt behaviour and how, for some people, it could be unlearnt. Interviewer, Piers Morgan, asked: "Do you know what we call these people, Dr Davidson? We call them horrible little bigots in the modern world. Bigoted people who actually talk complete claptrap and, in my view, a malevolent and dangerous part of our society." Morgan continued: "How can you think that nobody's born gay and they all get corrupted and they can all be cured? Who are you to say such garbage?" Davidson pointed out that neither the American Psychological Association nor the Royal College of Psychiatrists believed that homosexuality was always unchangeable. Then Morgan repeatedly shouted, "Shut up you, old bigot" as he brought the interview to a close.[128]

Jayne Ozanne would unlikely be spoken to in such an appalling manner. Who is being the bigot here? It is no more acceptable to meet Davidson's perspective with virulent abuse than any other viewpoint. No one seeking to forbid *Voices of the Silenced* had shown that either Davidson or his colleagues were forcing unwilling participants to acquiesce to a programme of heterosexual conversion. Piers Morgan was unlikely to have had any evidence as to how Davidson's 'counselling' was being carried out. Davidson said that some behaviour might be unlearnt. Douglas Murray guesses that:

> ... a set of assumptions are made about his [Davidson's group] and words assigned different interpretations because of their speaker. In this calibration 'voluntary' meant 'forced', 'counselling' meant 'persecution' and everybody who went to him [Mike Davidson] was irrevocably and unalterably gay.

Shown perhaps by Morgan, there has been the swift move towards:

> ... expressing opprobrium to anyone whose views fall even narrowly outside the remit of the newly adopted position. The problem with this is not just that we are at risk of being unable to hear positions that are wrong, but that we may be preventing ourselves from listening to arguments that may be partially true.[129]

Suggestions that all homosexuality is acquired and can be unlearnt may look as rigid and absurd a belief as that it is all innate and unchangeable, as with the shop-worn argument: "You're born gay!" versus "Nobody is born gay!" Here Christopher Rosik mentions how the "hyperbole on these issues" includes "scientifically uninformed comments by some leaders of the religious right...". This is unhelpful and "does damage to how this work is seen by the public and makes a reasoned discussion around these issues more difficult".[130] While one belief may adhere to some absolute genetic propensity, the other often makes claims about parent-child relationships being a primary cause of homosexual orientation.

Both views appear to be unfalsifiable, particularly given the ways in which they may be employed. One perspective may nod to developments in neuroscience (which relate to genes and brain structure), the other to re-worked Freudian legacies. There is no consensus on causation. If sexuality is fixed by biology, then conversion therapy is pointless. If not, and there is a likely mixture of nature and nurture, there is little reason why a person should be prevented from trying to change an aspect of their self.

Even within organised psychology, there may be "polarization ... over SOCE" leading to insularity "that treats one subgroup of sexual minorities as representative of the whole population, with detrimental consequences for accurately comprehending the complexities of sexual orientation change ...".[131] This impedes investigation. Reality is complicated, where there are suggestions that extreme experiences can change the expression of genes (epigenetics). So far, evidence points to some sexual fluidity, which is probably affected by both nature and nurture, which varies individually. There is:

> ... the possibility of multiple aetiologies or subtypes of non-heterosexual orientation, in which case it is quite possible that some persons may be able to transition from one sexual orientation to another without much difficulty, but that for other sexual minority persons, whether for innate or psychological reasons, change is difficult to impossible.[132]

Those who think that:

> ... nobody's born gay ... may be right or right in part. Nobody is yet certain. And whether or not anyone is born gay, or whether everyone who is gay is born gay, it does not follow at all that being gay is a one-way street.[133]

In *The Times* magazine, Emily Sargent describes how she set out to see if conversion therapy could cure her lesbianism. She contacted Mike Davidson, from CIT, who put her in touch with one of his counsellors, with whom she booked a course of six hour-long sessions. From the start, Sargent is implacably negative and oppositional, emphasising that there is no possibility that she is going to come out straight. She then carries out a hatchet job to "expose" a well-meaning woman, who is lied to and led to believe she is dealing with a 'conflicted' patient. The whole escapade is a sham from the start to denigrate 'conversion therapy' practitioners, along with any notions of sexuality change or fluidity. It is highly unlikely that this newspaper would publish reports from people who are genuinely seeking therapy to resolve their internal conflicts, or accounts of individuals who claim to be 'ex-gay', or a set-up where someone straight pretends to be confused about their sexuality and goes for help to someone who is a passionate LGB advocate.

Sargent uses her experience to corroborate "a vast amount of evidence to show that conversion therapy practices not only don't work but are deeply harmful, leading to depression, anxiety, self-harm and suicide attempts". In her "six sessions, as a happily 'out' lesbian, I could see that this was a deeply traumatising practice" where it was "harrowing to look at myself through the eyes of someone who thinks I am broken". This is hardly valid, confirmatory evidence, but then she believes there is nothing more to be found, since the Ozanne Foundation, with help from the Government Equalities Office (with David Isaac, from Stonewall, in charge) "confirmed [to her] where these practices happen, the forms they take, and the severity of the psychological damage caused".[134]

Empirical understanding is low on both sides here. Emily's therapist resorts to "methods based loosely in psychodynamic treatments" or digs around to find the "wound" or trauma in a "damaged" parental relationship, or a comment or move made long ago. Any imperfection in early relationships can be related to any later problem; *post hoc, ergo propter hoc* – after this, therefore because of this. Otherwise, if a suitable cause cannot be found, there must be something 'repressed' to fish out or invent to use as the reason for a hypothetical affliction that must be healed. All is unfalsifiable and therefore unscientific. This does not otherwise deny the effects of learnt behaviours or formative associations and experiences. Preoccupied with 'gay-cure', Sargent is seemingly oblivious to this aspect.

Whatever the beliefs of client or therapist about whether sexuality or gender identity is fixed, if someone believes that they have been affected by particular experiences, nothing should prevent them having an opportunity to discuss this without the risk of the practitioner being struck off, cancelled or criminalised.

Previously mentioned are how actual or prospective professional and official bans, along with activist outrage, make it difficult to investigate anything in an area where only the narrowest spectrum of views is permitted. Available, trustworthy data is thin on the ground and what passes for knowledge in the public sphere can be exceptionally poor. It is well said that, in "the absence of evidence, it would be proper scientific procedure to acknowledge one's ignorance." And, as knowledge stands at present, even "the involvement of some biological influence does not prove that change in sexual orientation is [always] impossible".[135]

Recently, there were calls from LGBTQ specialists to ban the publication of a large scale, genome-wide association study on 477,522 individuals which examined the genetic basis of same-sex behaviour.[136] Whatever the results, the prediction was that it was "going to be deliberately misused to advance agendas of hate". Fixed or 'born that way' could to some be as unacceptable 'as all can change', with fears:

> … that evidence that genes influence same-sex behavior could cause anti-gay activists to call for gene editing or embryo selection, even if that would be technically impossible [sic]. Another fear is that evidence that genes play only a partial role could embolden people who insist being gay is a choice and who advocate tactics like conversion therapy. "I deeply disagree about publishing this", said Steven Reilly, a geneticist and post-doctoral researcher who is on the steering committee of the institute's L.G.B.T.Q. affinity group, Out@Broad.[137]

4. Spiritual help?

Faith-based bodies might be high on the prohibition list as purported purveyors of 'coercive and abhorrent' practices. In early 2022, 55-year-old Chris Butler tells the BBC that he had suffered 12 years of "trauma" after "gay conversion therapy" when he was 19. Church elders purportedly pinned him to the floor, put a huge Bible on his head and performed an exorcism! With psychiatric measures disallowed or difficult to access, spiritual measures could be much of what is left on offer to help people. Often incorporating aspects of various psychotherapies, there are varieties of spiritual procedures related to sex and relationships which may be delivered within church groups.

These are likely to be delivered in more overtly devout religious settings. In what have become pro-LGBT social environments, religion may be a significant reason for individual decisions to seek orientation therapies.[138] Irrespective of the hyperbole, to *how many* therapy clients overall might this apply? In the study of reasons provided by a large representative sample of psychiatric practitioners, these claimed that religious beliefs only applied to 7% of clients seeking help, and social pressures from family to 14%. Confusion about sexual orientation was at 57%. [139]

Are specifically religious measures, which religious clients might seek, of the type that Jayne Ozanne describes as what "conversion therapy" might "actually look like today", for instance, "if you went forward and asked for prayer because you were struggling with same-sex attraction, … people would come alongside and start praying" for you "to be heterosexual or chaste"? Like Baroness Helena Kennedy, she reiterates how: "prayer that focuses on ensuring someone conforms to a 'norm' causes untold damage, is degrading and leads many to contemplate taking their lives."[140]

It has been mentioned how people are expected to conform to many norms, including ones they dislike. What is the distinction made between ones that cause "untold damage" and those that do not, and where is the evidence for how this happens in this context, or as a result of prayer?

Boris Johnson did maintain that pastoral support in some churches would be protected, and the UK Government emphasised how private prayer would not be criminalised. It did not intend a ban to impact "everyday religious practice", and there should be "no doubt" that individuals will be able to access "support and counsel from religious leaders". Yet, it is precisely these informal or quasi-religious procedures which often surface when activists demand criminalisation. After all, prayer has a purpose.

Labour MP, Angela Eagle, complained: "This proposed loophole [for prayer] is so large, there would effectively be no ban on conversion therapy". Stonewall emphasises that it wants the government to "put forward a full legal ban that protects LGBTQIA+ people from all forms of conversion therapy in every setting."[141] Nancy Kelley, CEO at Stonewall, is emphatic, stating in defence of her stance:

> ... half of the conversion therapy practices that take place in the UK are faith-based ... any ban that has

loopholes for any type of practice – including religious practices – will leave vulnerable LGBTQIA+ people at risk of further harm. It's vital the UK government puts forward a full legal ban that protects LGBTQIA+ people from all forms of conversion therapy in every setting.[142]

Lord Herbert of South Downs has no place for any exemption on grounds of freedom of worship for "an abhorrence", and activists in Wales insist that the ban must include praying with people who ask for prayer about their sexuality. When any:

> … aim to erase or repress someone's sexual orientation or their gender identity, people are coerced into taking part and they do tremendous harm to people. We can't allow the idea that simply because something is called a religious practice it can do no harm. We don't allow hate speech. Where it does harm there has [sic] to be limits to religious freedom, and I think we have to be clear about that. [143]

Just because "hate speech" is disallowed, is this supposed to somehow substantiate claims about "tremendous harm" from religious practices? This is hardly evidence. Should there even be "hate speech" laws to begin with? Noted by proponents of bans like the authors of the GEO report is how, "legislation that applies only to health professionals is likely to have only a limited impact on ending conversion therapy", given how much "appears to take place in religious settings". Not least, this is where it is said that crafty "therapy providers may rebrand and change their public-facing message in response to criticism and legal restrictions".[144]

Would this mean that "any Christian leader who dared to question the LGBT orthodoxy that sexual or gender identity is absolute, or suggest that sexual behaviour should not be determined by our feelings … be breaking the law"? Where is a line to be drawn, when 'conversion therapy' stretches to dialogue perceived as oppositional to LGBT ideology? Indeed, Matthew Roberts holds that Christian teaching is "antithetical to the entire understanding of humanity on which LGBTQ is based" where our "desires define us". Here, contrary to Christian thinking, our 'sexualities' are "the foundation of who we really are" and as the "self is our deity, woe betide anyone who questions its supremacy". In Christianity, we are "not self-created beings" who look inwards for our being and "sever ourselves from the true ground of our humanity". The "conversion to which Jesus calls us is a conversion to a glory infinitely higher and better than anything we can find in ourselves" and, if conversion therapy "is to be banned, the only way to do it is to ban Christianity."[145]

Professional organisations have already acted against practitioners using prayer, even when requested by clients. Psychotherapist Lesley Pilkington was the first to lose her membership of the British Association for Counselling and Psychotherapy for purportedly trying to convert a gay client to heterosexuality. In a sting operation, described as "pivotal in the movement to ban the practice", journalist Patrick Strudwick pretended to be a Christian asking for help to overcome unwanted homosexual tendencies, which were making him depressed. It was mutually agreed that the counselling would be based on Christian principles, and he accordingly received prayer, plus 'regression techniques'.[146] He had a mission "to root out therapists and psychiatrists who are practising these techniques and ultimately bring an end to them through exposing them, as well as disrupting their meetings".[147]

There might be questions about whether an accredited psychotherapist should venture into religious territory – but again, how far would a ban stretch? Does it cover suggestions that going to church might be helpful to resolve somebody's anxieties or conflicts?[148] Strudwick had all religious perpetrators in his sights, registered therapists or otherwise.

Stories of 'pray the gay away' procedures may largely relate to 'diverse' church communities, or those on the Evangelical or Pentecostal wing, which emphasise the workings of the Holy Spirit and have an informal, participatory approach to worship. However, using notions of internalised homonegativity, Ozanne extended her condemnation beyond certain types of churches and network groups, to blame the Church of England itself for creating 'turmoil and pain' by not endorsing an LGBTI agenda, thereby perpetuating stigma and prejudice that precipitated health problems leading to 'lasting damage'.[149]

As it is, leaders from every major church in the UK have repudiated 'conversion therapy', on the grounds that Christianity need not be at odds with a minority sexual orientation or gender identity. Pastoral counselling claims to be largely for providing support to LGBTQ2+ individuals, rather than changing their sexual orientation or gender identity. In 2017, the Church of England's General Synod passed a resolution calling on the Government to end 'conversion therapy', to prevent vulnerable people from being subjected to any psychological therapies and 'potential' spiritual healing/abuse with the purpose of leaving same-sex relations. Nonconformists would not be covered by prohibitions from the Church of England, the Catholic Church or other leading Christian ministries.

Definition is difficult, given the variety of forms and spectrum of cases. Would it cover 'private' praying alone, with a prayer partner or as part of a prayer group? Or would it only cover the laying on of hands, or the exorcism that is represented by LGBTQ activists as the spiritual equivalent of electrocution? For Ozanne or Kennedy, it would be all of these. If private prayer is to be excluded, who decides what is private – the police, the Crown Prosecution Service, a court or Stonewall? When this is at the instigation of the person receiving the prayer, must they be prosecuted for asking? Could it also be "deeply damaging" to refuse to offer treatment, making people feel "unacceptable and wrong"? Those who request prayer do so because they do not want to follow a particular life path. If online, would prayer, by definition, be 'public' and therefore illegal, along with some Christian websites, forums and videos? Prohibitionists may insist that there are no private decisions here. They see people being pushed to participate in prayer as much as in any other "conversion therapy" setting and believe that such people must be saved from the misery that they are ignorantly bringing upon themselves.

How are prohibitions enforced when some may not take kindly to intervention or clampdowns? Will bans cover mosques and madrassas? In some communities or religious groups, will this mean that all attempts or nods towards change or 'conversion' are kept secret? Will the police seek these out? Will congregations joining in prayer for somebody asking for help with combatting sexual inclinations they believe are wrong and do not want, be invaded by the police or by activists?

How would a comprehensive prohibition fit with Government assurances about religious liberty being protected? When people voluntarily seek prayer in connection with sexuality or transgenderism, is it the priest or the supplicant who is subject to legal sanctions, or both? Where is the coercion or influence that prompts official involvement when a parishioner wishes for counselling in the context of their religion? When a community is unhappy with a member's apparent sexual predilections or gender confusion, who evaluates the presence or degree of their influence as 'coercive'? Where 'conversion therapy' must 'not be tolerated' and even prayer for resolution or change might mean a criminal record, does a priest simply listen to someone who may have problems or questions about sexual identity, without offering advice or expounding Christian doctrine? Is a non-affirmative approach to the supplicant's unwanted identity tacit 'conversion therapy'? What happens when someone is unenthusiastic, unsupportive of another's gender change or sexual inclinations?

When a priest withholds the appropriate guidance or information on sexual ethics from someone who has expressly asked for this, is there a failure of moral duty? More widely, does this mean a restriction on religious belief and service if guidance or preaching on Christian sexual ethics could contravene 'conversion therapy' bans? As the campaign against 'conversion' broadens to controlling opinion and understanding about sexuality and relationships, this could cover schools, clubs and more.

Humanists UK's call for bans on any activity with the intent to 'change or suppress' someone's sexuality or gender identity extends to restrictions on freedom of religion or belief, if LGBT people 'feel' they are being harmed. Prayer, pastoral conversations, religious courses and activities would be outlawed, since 'conversion' covers expectations about living by Christian beliefs. That "God made humans male and female, in his image" and sex is for "marriage of one man and one woman" are in the line of fire. This could extend to declarations of faith and recitations of creeds, effectively outlawing baptism, confirmation and church membership.[150]

Stopping religious groups from using spiritual 'conversion' practices deemed to be harmful clearly extends to overturning generally established sexual ethics about behaviour and relationships. In February 2022, a letter signed by more than 2,500 church leaders and pastors was presented to the former Equalities Minister, asking that a ban on so-called 'conversion therapy' not outlaw the ordinary work of churches. The website of the Stanley Road Baptist Church in Morecambe, Lancashire was suspended by its host firm Torrix because the pastor was a signatory. LGBT activists publicly shared the details of the signatories on social media, warning people not to attend their churches as it could be "unsafe". Jayne Ozanne publicly accused them of abusing LGBT people. Robert Mee, CEO of Out in the Bay, asserted that LGBTQI people were being attacked even if "attacks are more discreet and secretive and almost whispers, but they are still attacks on us". Society was regressing where we have "forgotten about the holocaust and how LGBTQI people were persecuted and killed – history is repeating itself".[151] Such outlandish claims might relate to how, as gender identity gets uncoupled from biological sex, it takes on:

> … an intangible soul-like quality or 'essence'. As a pure subjective experience, it may be overwhelming and powerful but is also unverifiable and unfalsifiable. If this identity is held to be a person's innermost core concept of self, then questioning the very existence of gender identity becomes equated with questioning that person's entire sense of being, and consequently risks being considered a threat to the right to exist, or even as a threat to kill.[152]

In an ostensibly conciliatory move, the GEO's Coventry researchers suggest that, in "addition to legislative measures to ban or restrict conversion therapy, policies could focus on developing constructive dialogue with religious groups". Along with affirmative interventions for wavering individuals, this is meant to "educate them about the harms of conversion therapy and encourage alternative approaches to pastoral guidance with LGBT people of faith that avoid the aspects most likely to cause harm".[153] Who, assuming superiority, would be sponsored to give this compulsory (?) education to "religious groups" or churches. Would it be LGBT organisations, given their influence over educational matters? This is in line with the re-education programmes of despotic regimes.

What is manifest here and elsewhere is a drive to impose particular views and discriminate against dissenters. Consistent with the Scottish Parliament's statement to forbid any change attempts for anyone in any setting, those campaigning for a comprehensive 'conversion therapy' ban seek to criminalise virtually anything other than total acceptance and reinforcement of particular sexual or gender identities, for child and adult alike.

Chapter Four

NO CHANGE: DAMAGE DONE?

1. All decided?

Loudly and frequently heard is how it is impossible to change sexual orientation or gender identity and how attempts to do so cause 'devastating' harm or 'lasting damage'.

The reality is an area of highly inconsistent and contested findings for actual change, whether complete, incremental or zero, and similarly for adverse or beneficial consequences. This overwhelmingly relates to issues of sexuality, there being little research available on change efforts in relation to gender identity, although it has not prevented adverse results being ascribed to this.

Drawing on 'minority stress theory', Canadian activists Kristopher Wells and Nicolas Schiavo emphasise:

> There is no credible research that indicates you can change a person's sexual orientation or gender identity, rather what research does tell us is these so-called change efforts can have devastating impacts on its victims, including increased anxiety, depression, self-hatred, compromised mental health, post-traumatic stress disorder, suicide or suicidal thoughts, and many other lifelong psychological and social issues. [154]

This might cover every mental affliction! Conveying the same message, the Coventry University researchers' GEO report emphasises how any change of sexual orientation or gender identity is impossible and 'change' or 'conversion therapy' in any shape or form is *ipso facto* harmful. While this references material from *Teen Vogue*, Stonewall and the Ozanne Foundation, it draws on nothing that is critical of the affirmation of sexual orientation or gender identity which it recommends as the answer to any problems. There is nothing about the unprecedented rise in youngsters with gender dysphoria seeking to transition sex, or about any possible link that this might have to affirmation-only approaches. Nor is there mention of the rising cases of those who, regretting their journey, seek to detransition. The leading researcher is Adam Jowett, Associate Head of the School of Psychological, Social and Behavioural Sciences and chair of the Sexualities Section of the British Psychological Society. His research interests are primarily LGBT+ issues. Impartiality might be expected to be scarce here. Nonetheless, the report from the Scottish Parliament's Equalities, Human Rights and Civil Justice Committee, references the "independent research from Coventry University" along with its primary source – Jayne Ozanne![155]

It is difficult to overlook how the Coventry researchers seem set on dismissing anything that may question some foregone conclusions. A government, moving to enshrine in law something with potentially significant consequences for freedom, should have sought more independent advice. The Coventry researchers take a rigid 'no change, cannot change' perspective and insist that there is "no sound basis for claims that conversion therapy is effective at changing sexual orientation or gender identity."

To back their case there are repeated references to the 2009 review from the American Psychological Association's (APA) Task Force on Appropriate Therapeutic Responses to Sexual Orientation. The APA's sceptical, but sometimes reasonably impartial stance is presented as resolutely and completely oppositional to any prospects of change. Although this made a general claim that "sexual orientation is unlikely to change":

> The available evidence ... suggests that although sexual orientation is unlikely to change, some individuals modified their sexual orientation identity (e.g., individual or group membership and affiliation, self-labeling) and other aspects of sexuality (e.g., values and behaviour). They did so in a variety of ways and with varied and unpredictable outcomes, some of which were temporary. For instance, in some research, individuals, through participating in SOCE, became skilled in ignoring or tolerating their same-sex attractions. Some individuals reported that they went on to lead outwardly heterosexual lives, developing a sexual relationship with an other-sex partner, and adopting a heterosexual identity. These results were less common for those with no prior heterosexual experience.[156]

Irrespective of whether change actually occurs to any degree, it is questionable whether the aim of therapeutic measures should be construed only in terms of categorical moves with success defined as "changing ... sexual orientation or gender identity". Nor does recognising that change is possible mean that everyone can change,[157] or that this form of psychotherapy endeavour is the only one to result in no or poor outcomes. Regardless of the client's ostensible problems and stated goals, any psychotherapy may result in no or poor outcomes.[158] For the Coventry researchers, those who "perceived conversion efforts to have been a failure, when believing that change was possible, reported blaming themselves" and are consequently distressed, though this might apply to people using all manner of therapies for all manner of reasons.

The Coventry stance also much resembles the imposition of a 'gay script' or an LGBT understanding of therapeutic goals, where people centre their identity and lifestyle on a particular sexual orientation. This becomes the 'true self' which must be embraced and lived out, not one aspect of personal being or experience, where people establish their broad sense of identity around many roles, identifications, attachments, responsibilities and interests.

A "kind of trump card" is recycled. This reiterates how "the formal pronouncements claim that there is no good evidence that such therapies are effective and that they have the potential to be harmful." Critic Christopher Rosik attributes this to a lack of "ideological diversity in the leadership" of mental health and medical organisations in this field of study, with "a left-of-center groupthink process when addressing contentious social issues, including those involving sexual orientation". There is a serious problem here for what should be a scientific enterprise. Not least, from the time of the 2009

APA report, this has had "an inhibitory influence on the production of diverse scholarship in areas such as same-sex attraction change". Psychiatric associations "cite one another in an almost symbiotic manner" without providing new information relevant to answering important questions. They determine what and how research is conducted, interpreted and transmitted. There is "no need to manufacture some sort of conspiracy here", as this naturally occurs when the leaders of mental health associations all share the same basic values and worldview.[159]

The Coventry researchers see reports of change as pretentious or simply how some individuals "may modify how they label their sexuality" or "change of sexual behaviour". These "might only be temporary" and, with some people good at fakery, they "become skilled at ignoring same-sex attractions and go on to lead 'outwardly heterosexual lives'". Others are said likely to be bisexual to start with. A question is: just what, if anything, would they recognise as authentic change?

Investigation here is certainly challenging. As the Coventry researchers concede, there are:

> … no randomised trials of conversion therapies. Evidence regarding whether modern forms of conversion therapies are effective at changing sexual orientation typically rely on surveys that retrospectively gather self-reported data regarding individuals' sexual orientation after the conversion therapy. Due to a lack of controlled prospective studies, a reliance on self-reporting, potential sampling biases, a lack of objective measures, a lack of follow-up data and the inclusion of various conversion therapy methods within studies …

published research does not meet scientific 'gold standards' for making robust claims about effectiveness.[160]

Mentioned earlier was how difficult it is to have randomly selected comparison groups exposed to different measures for this study area and how this militates against establishing replicable, longitudinal evidence about changes, harms or otherwise, related to interventions. Unfortunately, so much that passes for "evidence ... consists of anecdotes". Then there are the "very small sample qualitative studies of persons who currently identify as sexual minority", and since these studies fail to exhibit clear change then, almost by definition, this is meant to be proof that change is impossible.[161] Nonetheless, there have recently been improvements and attempts at better controlled studies using samples from population cohorts (see below) where subgroups with different experiences can be compared, followed up and checked over time. Nowhere should problems with investigation indicate that there can only be one conclusion, or that the presence of any limitations be justification for the complete dismissal of a study's findings.

Something else which is particularly prevalent here is how 'stress' or 'stressful experiences' are made synonymous with 'damage', with no proper diagnoses of short or long-term mental health, or other, problems. This is, of course, a time when, worked up by the media, any shock, surprise, hurt, disappointment, distress, grief, fear, challenge, insult, disturbing or strange event, sadness or unpleasant memory, big or small, objective or subjective, is described as a 'trauma' portending 'devastating' consequences. If this were so, it is astonishing that human beings ever coped with, let alone succeeded, at anything. This is not to deny the evidence that extreme stresses can have adverse effects, as in the body of work related to Adverse Childhood Experiences (ACEs) which include physical, sexual and emotional abuse, neglect and pronounced disruptions or threatening circumstances (often related to matters like insanity, addiction, violence and so forth). Many are associated, often in a dose-dependent way, with later mental and physical health outcomes, from heart disease to neurological and neuropsychiatric conditions.[162]

There may be what, at first glance, look like succinct, convincing statements of fact:

> That there is a growing body of evidence that stigma associated with minority sexual orientations and gender identities (manifested as prejudice and discrimination) is a major source of chronic stress that can have a variety of negative mental health consequences for LGBT people (including suicidal thoughts). [163]

Several assertions are being made. People with minority sexual orientations and gender identities are surrounded by such discrimination and prejudice as cause "chronic stress" where, imbibing this as 'stigma', gives rise to mental health problems that include suicidality. All is apparently supported by a "growing body of evidence". Each, along with the connections, requires proof. Furthermore, while it is stated that self-selecting samples or "qualitative research cannot robustly answer the question of whether conversion therapy is harmful", it is then claimed that these "provide some indication of why it might be experienced as such".

Minority stress hypotheses (see below) have been called into question for a while now – something the Coventry researchers should perhaps have known about. Their own GEO report claims to be "based on the best available evidence" and does include à number of (mainly US) studies published between 2000 and 2020 which focus principally on sexual orientation change efforts. They also recruited 30 individuals for their own qualitative enquiry, via social media plus "a wide range of stakeholder (e.g., LGBT, religious and healthcare) organisations and the use of fliers at several Pride festivals". Of the 30 "screened for eligibility", 20 claimed to have experienced conversion therapy within the last 10 years, and others between 10 and 20 years ago. Several were excluded as the "treatment they underwent did not aim to change their sexual orientation or gender identity".

The findings for the small, self-selecting or volunteer sample are based on retrospective self-reporting. Like similar studies, there is the bias given how those who may have changed could have excluded themselves from participating since they no longer identify as gay or lesbian, or associate with the 'gay community'. All the unscientific "potential sampling biases" are here together with a "lack of objective measures … lack of follow-up data and the inclusion of various conversion therapy methods", cited by the researchers themselves as obstacles to "making robust claims". This tallies with how the APA Task Force Report of 2009 is criticised for demanding "randomized, controlled research designs to prove efficacy and reject case studies of success", while being "quick to tout anecdotal accounts of harm in the absence of any controlled, representative research showing harm".[164]

The Coventry researchers' interviewees commonly reported therapies loosely based on psychoanalytical ideas and techniques, perhaps in conjunction with counselling, religious support groups, workshops or conferences, where objectives moved between pastoral guidance or support to full change. It is described how most "experienced no change in their sexual orientation or gender identity, perceived conversion efforts to have been a failure and subsequently went on to accept their same-sex sexual orientation or gender identity". (Successful cases may not have bothered to volunteer.) However, there are two identifying as heterosexual now married to the opposite sex: the woman is described as probably sexually fluid anyway. There is a man who no longer identified as gay but continued to experience same-sex attraction, along with several others reporting changes in their sexual behaviour. It is suggested that this might just be how people see their sexual orientation and therefore does not represent reality. "Some of these interviewees" – numbers unspecified – "considered conversion therapy to have been (at least partially) 'successful'". It is not clear whether these form part of how "a third reported experiencing some secondary benefits".

Otherwise, in the Coventry sample, when most "spoke in general terms about how the conversion therapy made them feel", some interviewees claimed to have "feelings of stigma and shame which undermined their mental health" or "negatively affected their self-esteem and … had left many feeling there was 'something wrong' with them". A high degree of religiosity is reported for purported 'conversion therapists', who might have reinforced or enhanced any sense of conflict between the client's faith and sexual orientation or gender identity. Accounts of depression and suicidality support the researchers' conclusion that exposure to change efforts is "associated with multiple negative health outcomes (including suicidal thoughts and suicide attempts)".

There were no checks for pre-existing suicidality and distress, no prior or subsequent psychiatric or medical diagnoses available for the interviewees, nor any indication of what their mental health was like before and after 'conversion therapy'. There is a routine failure of studies to distinguish suicidal behaviour before and after SOCE.

Also, from an empirical perspective, there are questions about whether those with mental health problems, or who are troubled, may be more likely to seek out conversion therapy and, when this does not help or meet expectations, experience heightened regret, anger and/or dissatisfaction. As this 'qualitative' study involved those with a story to tell, it cannot give a proper picture of the effects of any therapy.

There is little information about the third who claimed to have received benefits, apart from some respondents "experiencing a sense of belonging and connection with other men in the same situation." In some cases, "lasting friendships were formed with those they met at conversion therapy weekend retreats and a sense of community was formed outside of the conversion therapy context".

The Coventry researchers put this down as something that might be "documented for social support groups generally" and that demonstrates how "it is unlikely that sexual orientation change efforts provide any unique benefits ....". Such "perceived benefits" are simply what "could be attained through alternative therapeutic approaches that do not attempt to change a person's sexual orientation or gender identity", or through affirmative LGBT groups. This is in line with the consensus in social and medical practice that past or present LGBT-identified persons must only be affirmed, even if it is to accept behaviours they do not want, or that they must be with those with whom they no longer wish to associate.

As reported, the bonds made in therapy were with "other men in the same situation ...". Human connectedness is important – often involving interpersonal relationships, with positive in-group identity or affinity which can support "more positive self-appraisals.[165] An inability to access social support from like-minded peers with similar goals might be detrimental to mental health, something which may account for some of the 'harms' otherwise reported in the Coventry study. The loneliness, alcohol and drug abuse, associated with social isolation may, indeed, be aggravated when there are aspects of the self some may wish to reduce or relinquish. That anyone might seek to do this is described here in terms of 'internalised homophobia' or influenced by the anti-gay prejudice imbibed from the person's surroundings.[166]

The Ozanne Foundation's *'Faith & Sexuality'* survey purports to be the first in the UK designed to understand the impact of religious belief on how people understand and accept their sexual orientation. This purported to "provide strong evidence of the harms that attempts to change sexual orientation are reported to inflict".

The participants were respondents to an online forum promoted by gay rights groups. Of the 458 out of 4600 who claimed they had experience of attempting to change their sexual orientation, 282 said it included "private prayer" or "prayer with close friends". No further definition of 'conversion therapy' was provided. Over half said they had experienced mental health issues, of whom nearly a third (91) had attempted suicide and over two-thirds suicidal thoughts, while others had self-harmed or suffered from eating disorders. There is no independent verification for these afflictions or what the sequence and connections could be, or who might have gone that way without the therapy. Few had sought advice from medical professionals.[167] Did those claiming 'attempted suicide' seek to end their lives, or were they imagining, planning or threatening this? Did they end up in hospital or were they rescued just in time and, if so, by whom and are there any records? Suicide 'attempts' may be a way of communicating distress, but often not necessarily the gateway to self-destruction that the conclusions claimed is commonly assumed.

Earlier, Ozanne's work had a critic complaining that this "provides not one shred of research evidence that demonstrates a link between conservative Christian teaching and mental health outcomes for LGB people".[168] With allegations that, apart from referencing each other, the Oasis group and Jayne Ozanne relied on anecdotes and offered no proof of the "abuse" in the churches and networks that Ozanne described, or how this equated with "teaching on the Holy Spirit", what should any proposed 'safeguarding measures' be safeguarding against? There is the conundrum that when someone seeks change for what they wish to remove or alter, what sets out to help them may, almost unavoidably, reinforce the notion of a problem or unwanted condition. Is any resultant harm due to the initial discontent or to the therapy itself?

People may blame themselves for their failure to move away from something they dislike, rather than question the efficacy of the help they received or even their possibility of change. However, when interviewees in the small GEO sample attributed feeling unhappy to the 'homosexual lifestyle' that they wished to leave, instead of the therapy they underwent, the researchers put this down to "internal conflict and internalised stigma". Is the suggestion here that those who wish to leave a homosexual lifestyle have a mental affliction which, if somehow alleviated by LGBT affirmation, will mean that they stay?

Even if the possibility of reconciliation to homo/bi-sexuality or gender change is welcomed by some, others might be disappointed or distressed when cajoled or 'converted' into closer identification with a particular lifestyle or tendency that they did not want. No attempt is made to justify refusing people's right to try and leave something which they do not want. Denying individual freedom of choice and leaving people to live with what they wish to relinquish, could be denounced as 'coercive and abhorrent'.

'Internalised stigma' is commonly understood as identifying with societal stereotypes, along with internalising shame, blame, hopelessness, guilt and fears of discrimination. It originally arose in relation to mental illness, where people with psychiatric health problems may experience shame at the diagnosis and the prospect of rejection.[169] From here it has been extended to explain problems affecting sexual and other minorities in terms of society's discrimination and shaming.

There has been a systematic literature review of the relevant databases to rate the available means for measuring 'internalised stigma'. Using standard quality control criteria for testing psychometric properties, the eight health conditions involved ranged from HIV/AIDS through mental health to obesity. Overall, of the 21 papers out of 33 that could be tested for scientific validity, only two received any positive ratings for quality criteria – namely, the Child Attitude Towards Illness Scale and Internalised Mental Illness Stigma.[170]

Should disliking aspects of oneself or one's sexual preferences or predilections be related to mental health considerations, or some form of aberration? It has been put forward by some pro-LGB researchers that investigation should focus on issues related to social wellbeing, in addition to studying the effects of stigma on mental disorder, given how: "People can think highly of themselves, be in good psychiatric health, but also be dissatisfied with their quality of life."[171]

Leading researchers set out to study the mental health effects of social stress burdens in a community sample of 396 self-identified LGB adults. Not least, findings were that "psychological distress and impaired wellbeing cannot be thought of as synonymous". Although women had more depressive symptoms than men, they did not have lower levels of psychological wellbeing, and Black LGB respondents did not show higher levels of either depressive symptoms or lower levels of wellbeing than their white counterparts. The frequently found coping mechanisms, such as community connectedness and self-esteem, mitigated any adverse mental health effects of stress. Bisexual and young respondents had lower levels of social wellbeing than their counterparts, even when they did not differ for psychological wellbeing and depressive symptoms. They may have difficulties in achieving social integration relative to other LGB persons, with lower levels of community connectedness and limited social support from other bisexuals.

Psychological wellbeing might relate to individual characteristics as much as social resources or support for sexual minorities, reflecting idiosyncratic factors. Here, and at odds with the common linking of social conditions to matters like depression, this was also found to be strongly rooted in individual vulnerabilities.[172] The findings are consistent with others that challenge minority stress theories.

2. Difficulties with Damage

Reliable findings for change, complete, incremental or none, and adverse or harmless associations, are scarce. When researchers in 2008 examined the scientific rigor of the "studies supporting the conclusions claimed by both sides" in the sexual reorientation therapy research, they found that this was "full of omissions which threaten the validity of interpreting available data". Primitive as it was, "any decisive claim about the benefits or harms really must be taken with a substantial grain of salt".[173] Much might be attributable to the samples selected for study and the outcome measures used. Those convinced of 'no change' might favour samples skewed towards respondents who have failed to change on any sexuality dimension. It may be the reverse for others who expect success and no harms from change efforts, although such researchers are thin on the ground, including in the UK. The Coventry researchers for GEO appear to disparage and dismiss results at odds with their views, while not levelling the same criticisms at others more in tune with their perspectives.

Depending upon the methodological level of investigations, this does not mean that researchers cannot, or do not, experience results contrary to their expectations or wishes. How these might be interpreted or explained is another matter. Nor does it mean that results supportive of researchers' views are not reliable – again, this depends much on the methodological quality. Validity ultimately rests upon the standards met by researchers, or how competently they use their methods and report their findings – not their opinions. All propositions and findings must be falsifiable or open to disproof.

One early US study (2003) to investigate reports of change (in attractions, behaviour, fantasy, yearning) from homosexual to heterosexual attributable to 'reparation therapy' and which lasted at least five years, interviewed 200 self-selected individuals (143 males and 57 females).[174] The majority reported moves from a predominantly or exclusively homosexual orientation towards a heterosexual orientation. Accounts of complete change were uncommon and female participants reported significantly more than males. (The researcher Robert L. Spitzer was instrumental in the American Psychiatric Association's decision in 1973 to remove homosexuality as a mental illness listing from the Diagnostic and Statistical Manual-III.) Spitzer suggested that these accounts either represented actual change or that some gay men and women constructed elaborate self-deceptive narratives or lied.

The study provoked considerable outrage. Spitzer backtracked and admitted that there was no way of knowing if the participants' accounts of change were valid. He apologised to "any gay person who wasted time and energy undergoing some form of reparative therapy because they believed that I had proven that reparative therapy works with some 'highly motivated' individuals."[175] The suggestions of self-deception or fabrications then made several of the original study participants challenge Spitzer's implied impugning of their integrity by alleging that the absence of a way to judge the credibility of respondents was a 'fatal flaw'.

They pointed to how "every other psychology study using self-report has the same limitations [this would include the 2021 GEO one], yet their authors do not apologise for their findings". Checks appeared to vindicate the self-reporters' credibility.[176] This has not prevented the study being repeatedly flagged up as disproof for any possibilities of change.

The new century was seeing:

> … a steady decline of such published studies … as the professional political climate has made such research professionally threatening, research funding and other support for such research has evaporated, and as the mental health professions have increasingly accepted various sexual orientations.[177]

Researchers were reporting how accusations of homophobic bias were serving "as an effective *ad hominem* argument that has undermined the credibility of this research".[178]

This might describe responses received by a quasi-experimental longitudinal study spanning 6-7 years which examined attempted religiously mediated sexual orientation change. It addressed the "questions of whether sexual orientation is changeable, and whether the attempt is intrinsically harmful, by focusing only on the religiously mediated approaches to change …". This initially recruited 72 men and 26 women who participated in 16 various ministries affiliated to Exodus, an umbrella organisation for people experiencing unwanted sexual attraction or sexual identity concerns. These ministries claim to neither reject homosexual persons nor embrace gay identity as an acceptable norm but aim to help those seeking to leave homosexuality through worship, prayer, education and discussion. The average age of participants was 37.5 years and the sample had considerable overall sexual experience (one third of the male sample had had sex with 30 or more other males). There was a retention rate of 64%; leavers may have re-embraced a gay identity or believed themselves free of homosexual inclinations and did not want reminders or were uncomfortable with the procedures.[179]

A range of qualitative and quantitative measures of sexual attraction, along with composite measures of sexual orientation and psychological distress, were administered longitudinally. This was arguably the best conducted study to-date of subjects seeking change through religious means, although there was no capacity to standardise or control actual intervention methods. A successful heterosexual adjustment is reported for 23% of the sample, along with 30% who experienced a reduction in homosexual attraction and reported stable chaste behaviour or a shift in self-identity rather than a change of orientation. There was no support for the hypothesis that involvement in the orientation change process "should result in worsening psychological distress outcomes", since psychological distress and psychopathology, by clinical measures, did not increase due to the change process; there were improvements on some measures.

Those who join up for change procedures have, in some sense, already rejected a LGB identity. The researchers speculate that change may be possible for some, but unlikely for all. With the right help and sustained commitment, people may be able to move along a continuum of decreasing homosexual behaviour and interests. Like Spitzer, the researchers worked at a time of mounting pressure from increasingly aggressive and well-placed identity lobbies that were making such research uncomfortable. In the face of mounting criticism, methodological limitations were explored that might restrict any generalisability of the findings or suggest alternative interpretations, with acknowledgements that the investigation did not "meet a number of ideal standards". The most pessimistic prognostication of outcomes in sexual outcome change was made by counting all missing cases as failures and success as total change on every measure. This yielded 9 per cent.

This might sit uncomfortably with Coventry University's GEO researchers' insistence on 'no change, much damage'. They found the Exodus study claims to be "unpersuasive due to methodological problems including the absence of a control or comparison group".[180] However, this also applies to their 30-volunteer sample. As they themselves acknowledged, randomly selected comparison groups are more or less impossible for this study area. However, there are recent developments to circumvent this problem.

Cited by the Coventry researchers as solid evidence of the harms of conversion therapy is an investigation using the 'generations' survey conducted by the Williams Institute (Berkeley, California), which provides demographic and socio-economic information about LGBT people in the US.[181] This used calls to 366,640 Americans to obtain a sample of 3,525 eligible LGBT participants, of which 1,518 (43%) completed usable interviews. These comprised three cohorts of sexual minorities in 2016: persons aged 52-59, 32-41 years and 18-25, amounting to a large, credibly representative sample of sexual minority persons. They were asked to rate their current health and sexual identity – lesbian, gay, bisexual, queer, pansexual, asexual, and other – together with sex 'assigned at birth' and current categorisation.

Approximately 7% had experienced SOCE (over 80% from a religious leader) over life. These tended to be the less affluent or educated, more black and male. Exposure went with far higher odds of all aspects of suicidality, like ideation, plans and attempts.[182] Leading researcher for the study was John Blosnich, director of the Center for LGBTQ+ Health Equity at the Suzanne Dworak-Peck School of Social Work in California, with a particular focus on social determinants of health. Another researcher was the leading exponent of minority stress theory (MST), which attributes harm to the effect of stigma, discrimination, and other 'homophobic' social stresses.

There are problems here that the Coventry researchers should perhaps have considered. Yes, the particular "strengths of this study include its random (probability-based) sample". However, the higher prevalence of suicidality was over lifetime. Without controls for existing suicidality, there is the possibility that the subjects sought SOCE because they were already troubled or had higher suicidality, rather than that SOCE caused harm. The study would have excluded any who might no longer identify as LGBT, whether or not SOCE had been received. SOCE therapy is usually for less than a year. Failure to allow for pre-existing suicidality might invalidate the conclusions (something the researchers re-examined).[183]

Back in 2015, the point was made that without "good quality outcome research, of which none exists, we have no way of disentangling pre-existing suicidality and distress from that which is allegedly caused by the therapy".[184] Studies may be violating the principle of temporal precedence – where the cause must precede the effect in cause-effect relationships, not *vice versa*. In turn, correlation alone is not causation. This applies to those quoted to demonstrate how "exposure to sexual orientation change efforts is consistently associated with higher likelihood of suicidal thoughts and suicide attempts compared to LGB people who have not undergone conversion therapy."[185] These may fail to distinguish suicidal behaviour before and after SOCE and, arguing from a lifetime of psychological morbidity, claim that SOCE induces harm.

There is a 'non-probability' survey of Canadian sexual-minority men, where about 3.5% reported having ever been exposed to SOCE. These were more likely to be gay than bisexual or transgender, and to be members of racial minorities and with lower incomes than non-participants. Exposure to SOCE was positively associated with loneliness, regular illicit drug use, suicide ideation and attempts. This research was used to support the proposition that all "levels of government in Canada should consider action to ban SOCE" and provide special support for 'survivors'.[186]

Similar considerations arise for the reference to transgender individuals made by the Coventry researchers. This involved a US-based self-reporting study of attempts to 'convert' transgender people to 'cisgender', that is, their biological sex.[187] Among the 71.3% who had spoken to a professional about their gender identity, around a fifth reported exposure to SOGICE (sexual orientation and gender identity change efforts) by professionals or religious advisers over lifetime. Their 'recalled exposure' was associated with severe psychological distress during the previous month and higher odds of lifetime suicide attempts. There is no data regarding the duration, degree, or forcefulness of any therapy, what techniques were used for this self-selecting sample or what their mental health states were before engaging in SOGICE.[188]

Then there is the matter of adverse childhood experiences. A previous review had systematically analysed 73 (mainly US) studies that addressed different types of adverse childhood experience and household dysfunction for non-heterosexual or transgender populations. Included is reported childhood sexual, physical and emotional abuse, along with neglect and caregiver problems like alcoholism, substance abuse, mental illness, incarceration and domestic violence. Exposure to such early adversities was higher than for heterosexual controls and related to increased rates of psychiatric symptoms, substance abuse, re-victimisation and dysfunctional behaviour.[189] Other work finds adverse child and adolescent experiences in terms of documented sexual abuse (not physical abuse or neglect) to be associated with later male same-sex relationships.[190] However, controls for one possible driver of afflictions does not account for all of these, or leave them attributable to SOCE.

A thorough re-analysis of the Williams Institute 'generations' data by other researchers has demonstrated that SOCE, if anything, was associated with reduced suicidal ideation, plans and attempts, with stronger effects for adults than juveniles. Over half of those who experienced SOCE had pre-treatment suicidality, while post-SOCE suicidal ideation odds went down by two-thirds for adults and one-third for minors. Suicide attempts were also reduced for post-SOCE adults, but less so for juveniles. Suicide ideation was less likely to lead to an attempt for both adults and juveniles when this was followed by SOCE.[191]

Suicidality harms attributed to SOCE exposure were reduced for its recipients compared with those for sexual minorities who had never engaged in SOCE. The previous researchers had considered (some) adverse childhood experiences (ACEs), and, as seen, research has suggested that childhood maltreatment can be related to mental afflictions by affecting brain development to some extent, perhaps in relation to underlying vulnerabilities.[192] Other precipitating factors or co-morbidities that might account for harms were not examined, including alcohol dependence, substance abuse, self-harming, poor mental health, psychological distress and suicidality – all of which were measured in the original 'generations' data. Several variables captured indicators of other stressors that might be related to SOCE or not, along with lifetime and current discrimination experiences due to minority sexual orientation. There are also chronic strains or personal stress conditions, such as isolation, exhaustion or conflict, not specifically related to any sexual orientation or gender identity.

In the re-analysis of the Williams Institute 'generations' data, multiple well-validated measures showed how the experience of SOCE was unrelated to present harms, including higher psychosocial distress or discomfort with an LGB sexual identity. There was no discernible psychosocial risk for those for whom SOCE had no efficacy compared with the non-SOCE group, despite higher lifetime stresses such as more adverse childhood experiences (ACEs), and a lower socioeconomic status.[193]

There are suggestions that the measures developed by the 'generations' study may still not capture all forms of adverse sexuality-related experience for those who engaged in SOCE. There are also the claims of greater concealment among SOCE recipients which are attributed to shame. Upon investigation, the opposite was found, as these were more likely to be unconcealed ('out') about their sexual minority identity, whether to family, friends, co-workers or healthcare providers.

It is open to debate whether the SOCE question was too narrow and prescriptive in asking: "Did you ever receive treatment from someone who tried to change your sexual orientation?" The goal of many SOCE practitioners might be to resolve psychological distress or conflicts related to same-sex attractions, behaviour, or identification. This may or may not involve seeking to modify elements of the client's sexuality. Therapy may be seen as SOCE or 'conversion' if it is simply open to the possibility of changing sexual orientation. In fact, almost half (49.1%) of those who answered "Yes" to the SOCE involvement question did not agree with the statement: "I have tried to stop being attracted to people who are the same sex as me."

Whether or not the later study of the 'generations' data would be validated or repeatable, the pressure continues for bans on SOCE based on claims about associations made with higher lifetime morbidity. While significant research which challenges dominant perspectives on any relevant or important issue should normally receive attention or examination, this appears unlikely to prevail here.

It can be overlooked that therapeutic procedures may help those of any identity or sexuality independently of the theories that their practitioners might have in relation to the ills of their clients, and irrespective of their intentions – big, small or none, for any changes to orientation.

One study tested the efficacy of cognitive behavioural therapy (CBT) to improve depression, anxiety, and co-occurring health risks (i.e., alcohol use, sexual compulsivity, condomless sex) among 63 young adult gay and bisexual men.[194] ESTEEM (Effective Skills to Empower Effective Men) is a 10-session intervention based on the Unified Protocol for the Transdiagnostic Treatment of Emotional Disorders.[195] It is individually delivered CBT designed to enhance the regulation of emotion; reduce maladaptive cognitive, affective and behavioural patterns; and improve motivation and self-efficacy across psychosocial problems. This promotion of personal agency and resilience was in a generally LGB affirmative context.

Convinced that problems suffered by their subjects were consequences of socially "imposed minority stress", the researchers also adapted the research protocols to help "identify minority stress experiences; track cognitive, affective, and behavioral reactions to minority stress"; and make sure that these "attribute distress to minority stress rather than to personal failure". The measures covered were: lack of support from family or security at work; anxiety about being rejected in 14 vignettes or particular experiences; being troubled about sexual identity and concealing sexual identity. Participants indicated the degree to which they were "out of the closet" in five domains: family; gay, lesbian, and bisexual friends; straight friends; co-workers; and health care providers. The group was divided into two, where only one received the additional interventions that addressed gay stresses along with the CBT programme.

Participation in CBT significantly and meaningfully reduced depressive symptoms, anxiety symptoms, alcohol problems, sexual compulsivity, condomless anal sex with casual partners, and improved condom use self-efficacy. Little showed that any problems were related to specifically gay-related stresses. This might be reinforced by the consequent study which "tested the efficacy of a minority-stress-focused cognitive-behavioural treatment" for two groups of sexual minority women dealing with "depression, anxiety, and alcohol use problems". While there might have been significantly reduced depression and anxiety, and a marginal reduction of alcohol problems, any minority stresses were minimally affected and questions are raised over measurement and stresses within lesbian communities.[196]

Disappointment is very apparent for the first study's weak changes for minority stresses, despite the additional therapeutic measures. There are explanations for why the expected results for problems "such as sexual orientation concealment and internalized homophobia" did not occur. It is surmised that:

> ... the minority stress measurements, such as sexual orientation concealment and internalized homophobia, may have suffered from range restriction given the fact that the young gay and bisexual men in this study were relatively open and comfortable with their sexual orientation, living in an urban center, and mostly recruited through gay-specific venues.[197]

Perhaps they did not have problems with stigmatisation in the first place. Again, while participants might have had mental health problems and sexual risk behaviours, they were not "necessarily experiencing minority stress". As young gay and bisexual health conditions had improved, there are recommendations for "larger sample sizes ... to detect significant changes in the minority stress and universal processes that are hypothesized to underlie these conditions [of poor health]". It might be hoped that, with a greater number of participants, the greater are the chances of finding what you are looking for. If you manipulate the sample enough, it might deliver.

Studies of any association between sexual orientation concealment (seen as an important indicator of minority stress and accompanying mental health problems) show contradictory results from positive through null to negative. A meta-analysis using 193 studies found a small positive association between sexual orientation concealment and mental health problems like depression and anxiety, with negative associations for substance use problems.[198]

Despite minimal or null evidence, advice for "modifying minority stress processes" has been for "more intensive intervention efforts, more time to manifest, and/or concomitant reductions in the societal conditions (e.g., discriminatory laws, policies and community attitudes) that drive minority stress at the structural level" for purportedly stigmatised groups. Here, "continuing to reduce structural stigma to eliminate sexual orientation health disparities represents an essential public health goal" because:

> ... according to minority stress theory, until structural stigma is completely eradicated, gay and bisexual men will continue to disproportionately experience mental health problems and associated psychosocial conditions relative to heterosexuals.[199]

To "promote structural change", the recommendation is "to empower marginalized individuals to establish that change ... empowering the mental health treatment community to provide evidence-based [sic], LGB-affirmative clinical services".

Continuing claims about 'structural stigma' towards LGBTs co-exist with full equality and even protected categorisation in law, along with immense celebratory events and media promotion. Not least in the UK, groups representing sexual and gender minorities have power throughout public and private bodies and their problems receive a considerable allocation of resources. From several perspectives, the notion of pronounced minority stress is questionable, and for some groups perhaps more than others.

3. The Most Damaging?

With the arrival of better controlled and often large-scale studies measuring different variables, so far, there are suggestions that SOCE attempts may not be the invariably 'damaging' experiences persistently proclaimed. Accusations of harm may originate in connection with interventions that are "inept, harsh, punitive or otherwise ill-conceived and not from the attempts to change itself". This can stray into the anecdotes about exorcisms and related activities that crop up with claims about 'coercive and abhorrent' experiences.[200]

Religious or spiritual procedures or connections have been those considered the most misguided and repugnant. This is significant, considering how important an influence on individual decisions to seek any reorientation or change therapy religious affiliation may be. There may be guilt or shame related to religious teaching, actual or potential rejection from others in the community, along with family pressure and a prospect of having to forsake one's religion.

Aside from actual 'change' procedures, religion may be presented as detrimental to LGBT or same-sex attracted people anyway. However, there is a whole spectrum of religiously or spiritually related measures which, along with a great diversity in approaches to human sexuality and relationships, may combine with various psychiatric and other services. For example, the doctrines associated with highly conservative or more orthodox churches may be used to characterise the general religious responses to homosexuality and transgenderism.

Information here principally relates to the US and to teachings and practices perhaps little present in the UK. Data from the 2018 Post-Midterm Election Study – a survey representative of adults in the USA aged 20 to 65 years – examined the social factors associated with approval or disapproval of hormonal and/or surgical interventions for adolescents seeking treatment for gender dysphoria. Evangelicals were most likely to oppose (81%), followed by Mormons (80%) and those saying religion is more important than anything else (80%). The politically conservative or very conservative come in at 70% and 72%; Pentecostals (69%); and attendees at weekly religious services (about 70%). Those most likely to agree with treatment were very liberal politically (72%), and likely to believe that "marriage is outdated" (52%) or did not completely identify as heterosexual (50%).[201]

There is little or no research which might compare the nature of SOCE procedures and outcomes across religious denominations. Nonetheless, what is available through surveys and convenience-sampled populations from religiously affiliated organisations may provide some useful information about the outcomes for variant change procedures if these are carefully investigated.

One sample of 125 US men underwent SOCE for homosexual-to-heterosexual change in sexual attraction, identity and behaviour, and to deal with psychosocial problems (depression, suicidality, self-harm, self-esteem, social function, alcohol or substance abuse). Participants were contacted mainly through religious organisations and therapy networks. Compared to the general male population, the respondents were disproportionately highly educated, affluent, with high levels of religious observance; most came from Christian denominations and 10% were Jewish. The leading resources used were from religious support groups (81.5%) and pastoral counsellors (70.2%), along with same-sex retreats, marriage counsellors, psychologists, psychiatrists and non-religious support groups.[202]

Exposure to SOCE was associated with significant declines in same-sex attraction, identification and sexual activity. While increased same-sex orientation measures were experienced by 4-10% of participants, between 45% and 69% achieved at least partial remission of unwanted same-sex sexuality. Full remission was achieved by 14% for sexual attraction and identification, and 26% for unwanted sexual behaviour. Rates were higher among married men, for whom maintaining and strengthening heterosexual marriage was a significant motivating factor in the decision to pursue SOCE. A previous investigation of what motivated men to seek

SOCE showed this to be being married, along with feeling disconnected from or conflicted over expressing nonsexual affection towards men.[203]

Marked or severely negative psychosocial change was reported for 4.8%, while 12.1% to 61.3% reported marked or very positive psychosocial changes for various dimensions, with net change significant for all measured domains. Positive change was strongest for depression, self-esteem, social functioning, self-harm, and alcohol/substance abuse, with nine times more (21.8%) positive effects of SOCE on suicidal thoughts or attempts than negative effects (2.4%). Apart from commitment and the apposite nature of the help received by participants, their common affiliations and interests may have provided empathy and understanding while avoiding the social isolation reported by some during and after change procedures.

Overall, SOCE was perceived as an effective and safe therapeutic practice, helping the participants to organise the sexual self more fully around heterosexual expression. The long-term prospects cannot be known or whether there is a short-term 'placebo effect' due to expectations of change. The researchers "caution against broad generalizations of our results", not least when samples are recruited via therapy networks. More benefits accrue where, along with shared religious values, there is empathy and support from interacting with others in similar circumstances. Whether the SOCE succeeded because the recipients had already reframed their sexual identity could be something applicable to many conditions; those voluntarily engaging in therapy want this to take away something they already see as a problem to be reduced or removed.

A comparison might be the poorer results for 1,612 current or former members of the Church of Jesus Christ of Latter-day Saints (LDS or Mormons) who claimed to have engaged in change efforts "at some point in their life". This has received attention as an exemplar of ultra-conservative religious tradition – credited with a staunchly doctrinal and administrative opposition toward same-sex sexuality, along with church-related familial and social pressure on members to eschew LGBT orientations.

Data here was obtained through an online, self-report survey.[204] Recruitment was via press and internet coverage, and major LGBTQ support groups (including explicitly non-religious organisations), and participants need not have aimed at full sexual orientation change. The purpose was "to document and evaluate the prevalence, variety, duration, demographics, effectiveness, benefits, and harm of sexual orientation change efforts within one particular faith tradition …". Factors associated with participating in SOCE included less family and community support for LGBTQ identities (for men), and high levels of early religious orthodoxy. There is great diversity here in relation to goals, religiosity (or the lack of it), persistence and commitment.

Only one participant out of 1,019 who engaged in SOCE for sexual orientation change attained a heterosexual identity according to self-reported sexual attraction and identity ratings. A further 32 described a decrease in the frequency and/or intensity of their same-sex attraction or behaviour, but no change in the definition of who they were. There might be acceptance of sexual orientation 'as God created me', with a decrease in depressive or anxiety symptoms, and improved family relationships. Religious (prayer, scripture study, fasting etc.) and private forms of SOCE were most prevalent, although 44% reported some form of therapist or group led SOCE. Aside from the LDS emphasis on prayer and consulting with church leaders to deal with unwanted same-sex attraction, there may be a greater need for privacy where there is apprehension of possible social disapproval.

In general, no significant difference in quality of life was found between those who either did or did not aim at full change of orientation, although men who engaged in SOCE to this end tended to have poorer psychosocial function, higher sexual identity distress and lower self-esteem. Some reported reductions in depression and anxiety or acceptance of same-sex attractions. Some felt they had wasted their time and money, alongside having increased their distance from the church, worsened family relationships and, with 'spiritual struggles', may have associated failure with feelings of unworthiness and abandonment by God. Outcomes varied greatly in relation to the reported goals and methods which, in turn, were very varied in form and quality. Psychotherapy and support group efforts of short duration were rated most effective and the private and religious-based efforts the least (these could run for years).

This is a rather chaotic study. The sampling limits the ability to generalise the findings to same-sex-attracted current and former LDS church members. It is possible that a significant number of both highly devout and highly disaffected current and former LDS church members were unaware or avoided participating. Others described their experiences as SOCE, even though they had not indicated "change" as either a goal or as something worked on.

Another study of 1,128 sexual minority Mormons from politically conservative or liberal circles found that the more seriously religious – who rejected an LGBQ identity but accepted same-sex attraction – were, perhaps unsurprisingly, less content with their sexuality, but had similar health outcomes to LGBQ accepting Mormons.[205]

People generally benefit from religious connections. Involvement in public religious practices is associated with generally lower levels of suicidality through the high levels of support provided by religious communities.[206] It cannot be assumed that a church or its membership is hostile to homosexual individuals, whatever the beliefs of people might be towards homosexual practices and relationships. One investigation, on the impact of religious affiliation and religiosity on mental health outcomes for Australian LGB adults, specifically found that suicidal thoughts had no association with religious affiliation.[207] In several studies, measures of religiosity across religious affiliations (e.g., Protestant, Catholic, Jewish, Buddhist), are unrelated to mental health outcomes for sexual and other minorities.[208]

Affiliation is one matter; degree of involvement another. While a study of a suicidal adolescent sample found no relationship between parent/adolescent religiosity and suicidal ideation for same-sex attracted youth, high religiosity was associated with more suicide attempts, but fewer for those reporting only opposite-sex attraction.[209] There are similar results for a sample of LGB individuals from New York City venues. Representativeness cannot be known.[210]

For another sample of 355 New York City LGBs from a 'community-based venue', the study's authors:

> ... hypothesized that exposure to non-affirming religious settings would lead to higher internalized homophobia, more depressive symptoms, and less psychological well-being ... that Black and Latino LGBs would be more likely than White LGBs to participate in non-affirming religious settings and would therefore have higher internalized homophobia than White LGBs.[211]

Results initially supported "the general hypothesis that non-affirming religion was associated with higher internalized homophobia" – or dislike with being homosexual – in the overall sample. However, this did not generalise to self-esteem. Latino, but not Black, LGBs had higher 'internalised homophobia' than White LGBs after controls, which related to their greater affiliation with non-affirming religious settings. Using the Center for Epidemiologic Studies – Depression (CES-D) scale (which is not an accurate measure of mental problems) 'internalised homophobia' or rejection of homosexuality initially seemed related to depressive symptoms and lower wellbeing. However, participation in non-affirming religious settings did not lead on to worse mental health outcomes. Instead, affiliation to a conservative church had a stronger effect of ameliorating depression and improving wellbeing than not being affiliated or being connected instead to a liberal church. Elsewhere, religiosity buffers the effects of perceived racism, and moderates the thoughts of suicide for African American adults.[212] Abandoning one's religion is found to be generally associated with ambivalent homosexuals having higher risks of depression and suicidality.[213]

There are interpretations of these results which highlight the countervailing effects of religion on LGB people in relation to social support and meaningfulness. Hence, LGBs "continue to participate in religious institutions that condemn" their behaviour "because they derive great personal meaning from the religious setting they have been accustomed to (often since childhood) … religious settings provide an affiliation and connection with a community … Leaving one's religious institution is socially, culturally, and spiritually discomforting …".[214]

In a further sample of 274 sexual minority subjects with diverse religious and sexuality labels, those who rejected an LGB identity were more likely to be religiously active, full members of their church, and theologically conservative in their religious viewpoint. Reported as having greater 'internalized homonegativity' and interested in child-centred family life, they were more likely to be single and celibate or in a heterosexual relationship. Contrary to expectations, the differences were not associated with depression, anxiety, or poor social flourishing, even though GB-identified participants reported higher life satisfaction than those rejecting an LGB identity.[215]

Illustrating how the costs of leaving a non-affirming setting might outweigh the stress of remaining are results from a large sample of 18-24 year olds recruited to investigate relationships between religious and sexual identity conflict, 'internalised homophobia' and suicidality.[216] Seventeen per cent matured in a non-religious environment; 40% reported a religious upbringing without experiencing religious and sexual orientation or identity conflict; and 43% had experienced conflict between their religion and sexuality. Unresolved conflict was reported by 12% of the sample, who were significantly younger than those with resolved conflict. Other researchers who found that younger LGB persons had the lowest social well-being compared to other age cohorts suggest that, despite having greater general acceptance compared to their predecessors, time is needed to form personal accepting and accommodating social environments and achieve reconciliation with surrounding norms.[217]

On average, the 18 to 24-year-olds had "a minimal level of internalized homophobia", even if this was higher for those who matured in a religious environment and/or whose parents were unsympathetic to homosexuality. Those at the higher level of the "minimal" had a larger incidence of recent suicidal thoughts, but there was no significant relationship with suicide attempts (reported by 3% of the sample). Leaving one's religion was associated with a decrease in internalised homophobia, but higher risks of suicidal thoughts and attempts. Hence "the negative impact felt from leaving ... has a stronger impact than the positive indirect impact through a reduction in internalized homophobia." The latter is weak compared to the harms to individuals from "isolation from communities of historical significance to the client (i.e., loss of community, potential loss of protective belief structure)".[218] Those who assume that someone could just leave their religion and 'come out', may not understand the dilemmas that such a person actually faces. Someone relates how he contemplated what might happen if he chose to identify and live his life as a gay man:

> I went down in my mind this path of finding a lover, leaving my wife, and losing everything I loved, which was my wife and my family and my church and my God, my relationship with Him, and not finding any real happiness in that relationship in my mind because by that point I had known other people who had been in these relationships and they were fleeting ...[219]

Pay-offs for moves in terms of accepting or taking on other liabilities is not uncommon in life. Perhaps seen here for members of stricter religious communities is how discomfort with homosexuality is balanced against the benefits otherwise bestowed by membership, even if this may be difficult for outsiders to recognise. It might need to be understood that "respecting religion as an aspect of diversity" means "respect for those who hold to the conservative, orthodox teachings of that religion".[220] This does not deny that there are those for whom neither gay-affirmative nor change therapy may be appropriate or possible. Instead, the practitioner may strive to resolve conflict between 'affectional orientation' and religious identity, and help clients integrate their conflicting religious and sexual selves. There might be 'sexual identity management', which can involve separating identity and expression, and perhaps making distinctions between the public and private, beliefs and behaviours, which enable a person to reach a healthy degree of self-acceptance. Another study, of 1,128 sexual minority Mormons from politically conservative or liberal circles, found that the more seriously religious – who rejected an LGBQ identity (gay, lesbian, same-sex attracted or questioning) but accepted same-sex attraction – were, perhaps unsurprisingly, less content with their sexuality but had similar health outcomes to LGBQ accepting Mormons. Research suggests that LGBQ individuals who successfully integrate their religious beliefs and their sexuality tend to have higher self-esteem, self-acceptance, and fewer mental health problems.[221]

The point is made that respecting religion and those who hold to conservative, orthodox teaching is itself an aspect of diversity. Therefore, to deny 'affectional reorientation therapy' is itself unethical.[222]

For some, like Humanists UK, saving people from 'harmful' circumstances, appears to involve bans covering basic Christian beliefs and routes to church membership. Choice, when it comes to faith, has no place here. As two groups confront each other with divergent value systems, each expecting the other to conform, it should be recognised that "psychology may not be able to change the doctrines of religion and that religion may not be able to change the intentions of LGB-affirmative clinicians and researchers".[223]

It cannot be assumed that, for everyone, sexuality should be the defining characteristic of a person or their life's focus. For activists that may well be the case. Otherwise, it may be "remarkable both conceptually and scientifically" to speak of people organising their lives around their sexuality or how this somehow encompasses their personal and social identity. One critic cannot conceive of data comprehensive enough to support this claim or understand how science could establish how such a grounding of human identity is 'positive' or even establish "a sexual orientation as a fundamental for constituting the self?"[224] What is normal or positive or legitimate in relation to these issues is more the domain of religion or philosophy than politics or legislation.

The prioritisation of sexual identity may relate to how established understandings of individual liberty have been cast as oppression, while freedom is equated with disengagement from any customary norms or from society itself. In this way of thinking, human beings are not socially rooted and sustained, but detached sovereign beings. Operating without structure or support, the individual is meant to fully create its version of culture and now, even re-make itself. There may be difficulty in understanding that, for those who seek to preserve the traditions and norms that underpin their past and present, the welfare of family and other social ties are important. Advocates of the ban on therapy may not recognise socially or communally based values and membership, and instead see only sources of oppression that, as such, do harm.

4. Change anyway?

Aside from the results of treatment to change sexuality and gender, does change happen anyway? Those out to prohibit 'conversion therapy' often insist that change is impossible. Is this no more likely to happen outside of 'change' targeted interventions than it can inside? Is this borne out by evidence? Otherwise, might people "with changing sexual attractions ... be reassured to know that these are common rather than atypical"?[225]

There have been numerous investigations into the flexibility of sexuality for both sexes, and these hardly suggest that this is entirely hardwired for everyone, as many people appear to move in and out of various attractions, practices and identifications. Both gender and sexual identities may emerge, change, or fade to a lesser or greater degree over life.

Longitudinal studies showing such variation in attraction and behaviour include the immense National Longitudinal Study of Adolescent to Adult Health (Add Health). This followed a nationally representative sample of over 20,000 US adolescents who were in grades 7-12 during the 1994-95 school years and followed for five waves to 2016-18.[226] Only 27% of respondents who indicated same-sex attraction in wave 1 reported this in wave 3, and 28% who reported a same-sex relationship later self-identified as entirely heterosexual. Analyses of three waves (6 years) of the National Longitudinal Survey of Adolescent Health data found that the prevalence for non-heterosexuality in matters like romantic attraction and identity varied between 1% and 15% and was higher for females. Migration over time among sexual orientation components is in all directions: from opposite-sex attraction and behaviour to same-sex attraction and behaviour and *vice versa*.[227] Even more than one in 12 of exclusively homosexually attracted males moved, often to exclusively heterosexual attraction.

Same-sex attraction is much more common than same-sex experiences or a same-sex identity, especially among women, as shown for a New Zealand birth cohort which examined differences by age and sex for changes in sexual attraction over several decades. For women, this doubled up to age 26 (to 16.6%), then decreased by age 38 (12.0%), whereas among men this was higher at age 38 (6.5%) than 21 (4.2 %).[228]

Similar results are shown for Britain, where 15,162 men and women aged 16-74 years, resident in a private household in Britain were interviewed between 2010 and 2012 (with a 57.7% response rate) for the third National Survey of Sexual Attitudes and Lifestyles. Overall, 2·5% of 16–74-year-old men and 2·4% of women self-identified as lesbian, gay or bisexual; 6·5% of men and 11·5% women reported any same-sex sexual attraction; 5·5% of men and 6·1% of women reported same-sex sex at any time, and a further 2·4% of men and 5·3% of women reported same-sex experience but no genital contact. Among those who were more often, or exclusively, attracted to people of the same sex, men were more likely than women to report exclusively same-sex experience (37·8% vs. 14·6%). Of those reporting same-sex sex in the past 5 years, 28% of men and 45% of women identified as heterosexual.[229]

Many with episodes of same-sex behaviour or attraction, particularly in their youth, will not go on to identify as gay, lesbian or even bisexual, or want to prematurely label themselves, as they may not equate this with having a homosexual or bisexual orientation or identity *per se*.[230] Others who might have both male and female partners call themselves heterosexual, just as some listing as same-sex have opposite sex partners.[231] In the 2020 University of Chicago US survey, 57% percent of people who identified as gay (40% of men and 78% of women) reported having had one or more opposite-sex sex partners since age eighteen.[232] Opposite sex partners at some point in life are not unusual for those with predominantly same-sex attractions, particularly lesbians.

These results are consistent with a study of self-reported change over time for sexual fantasy, romantic attraction, and sexual behaviour across three categories of current sexual orientation (heterosexual, bisexual, and gay). This involved 762 self-identified heterosexual, bisexual, and gay men and women, aged 36 to 60, via a self-report questionnaire. There were significant differences for changes in orientation for both homosexuals and heterosexuals, with women reporting greater change, while bisexual men and women did not differ.[233] It is not unusual to find that sexually involved young women who purport to be exclusively attracted to men are far more likely than those who are not sexually involved to engage in same-sex activity.[234] Again, women reported greater change than men.[235]

Men have been described as having a "category specific sexual arousal pattern, one that is usually directed much more strongly to members of one sex than to those of the other". In contrast, the arousal pattern of women tends to be bisexual, and irrelevant to most women's partner choices. Therefore:

> The category specific male sexual arousal pattern is the primary sexual motivation that directs male sexual activity to certain kinds of individuals (most often women, but sometimes men) rather than others ... a man's category specific sexual arousal pattern is his sexual orientation. Most women lack this strong directional motivation, and so it is not surprising that their sexual behavior is more malleable and sexually fluid.[236]

With sexual behaviour and diversity growing across generations, younger people have become significantly more likely to identify other than heterosexual and to say they are equally attracted to both sexes.[237] Across the 27 countries surveyed by the Ipsos LGBT+ Pride 2021 Global Survey, there is a wide generation gap around gender identity as well as sexuality. Those who identified as transgender, non-binary, non-conforming, gender-fluid, or other than male or female made up 4% of Gen Z (born since 1997) compared with 1% among all adults.

For the US, the percentage of people who identify as LGBT has roughly doubled each generation. Gallup's latest update (2021) has 7.1% of US adults identifying as LGBT; this is up from 4.5% in the previous 2017 data. As younger generations are more likely to consider themselves to be other than heterosexual, one in five Americans aged 18 to 23 in 2021, or nearly 21%, identified as LGBT.[238] This progressively lowers to less than 2% for those aged 56 or older. More than half of LGBT adults (54.6%) identified as bisexual; a quarter as gay (24.5%); 11.7% as lesbian; and 11.3% as transgender (respondents could give multiple responses when describing their sexual identification). The share of the total US adult population is 3.1% bisexual, 1.4% gay, 0.7% lesbian and 0.6% transgender. Of young adults, the vast majority (72%) of those who identified as LGBT claimed to be bisexual (amounting to 11.5% of all young adults, with about 2% each gay, lesbian or transgender).

An ever-increasing number of young people in the US have also identified as transgender and nonbinary. In the Williams Institute research, the figures doubled among 18 to 24-year-olds from 0.66% in 2016 to 1.3% in 2021. In addition, 1.4% of 13 to 17-year-olds identify as trans or nonbinary. These are said to be underestimates due to factors such as incomplete data collection for some states.[239] Further research finds that 2% of those aged 18-29 identify as transgender and 3% as nonbinary, far higher than in other age cohorts.[240]

Data from the UK's recent Annual Population Survey (APS) for 2020, shows a substantial increase since 2014 for sexual minorities, when estimates began for the numbers of young people aged 16 to 24 identifying as other than heterosexual or straight. This is a move from 2.1% to 3.3% for young males, and from 0.9% to 1.8% for young females identifying as gay or lesbian. In turn, 0.8% of males in 2014 and 3.1% in 2020 claim bisexuality compared with a move from 1.8% to 7.6% for females. Those describing themselves as 'other', move from 0.4%

and 0.4% to 1% and 1.6% respectively. Refusals and 'don't knows' are 4.2% (2014) and then 2.5% (2020) for males, and 3.5% then 3.4% for females; figures may not always add up due to rounding. Girls in this age group were on a par with males in 2014 when it came to reporting a heterosexual identity (93.2% to 93.5% for males and females). However, by 2020, the figures alter somewhat to become 88.5% and 86.2% respectively. This may suggest that bisexuality is more common among young females.

For the general UK population of all ages, 95% of males claimed a heterosexual identity in 2014 compared with 95.5% of females, with a shift to 93.2% and 94.1 % by 2020. In 2014, 1.5% and 0.3% of males claimed a gay or bisexual identity compared with 2.5% and 0.9% in 2020. The shift for females is from 1% and 0.7% to 1.1% and 1.6%. Unsurprisingly, London had the highest regional proportion of adults identifying as lesbian or gay or bisexual in 2020. Sexual identity does not necessarily reflect sexual attraction or behaviour, and these are not currently measures by the APS.[241]

It is suggested that more young people are combining recreational both-sex relationships with heterosexual relationships.[242] Along with the growth in partner numbers, and concurrent relationships reflected in statistics for the general UK population, between 1990 and 2000 the proportion of men reporting ever having had a male partner rose from 3.6% to 5.4%. Among people of all orientations, those running 'concurrent' partnerships (two or more at the same time) rose from 11.4% to 14.6%

for men (20% for 15- to 24-year-olds), and from 5.4% to 9% for women (15% for 15- to 24-year-olds).[243]

The greater volatility at young ages, especially for girls, may be manifest in how bisexuals are far more likely to go on and marry someone of the opposite than the same sex. Data from the Office of National Statistics (2016) had almost a quarter (24.9%) of bisexuals married to an opposite sex partner. Only 0.3% had a same sex spouse and 0.9% a civil partner. Amongst those aged 16-34, there were a third more female than male bisexuals.[244] Moving into heterosexual marriage may relate to sexuality changes with age. Several population studies across the Anglophone sphere show considerable movement, with 26%-64% of same-sex attracted respondents reporting change which was overwhelmingly towards heterosexuality.[245]

There is the question of whether younger people answer honestly to interviews or are "exaggerating their sexual versatility because these days (and in some social circles) that's the cool or fashionable thing to do – swinging both ways being thought more liberated and fun than confining yourself to one sex". In an increasingly sexualised world where people are engaging in sex at an earlier age, with more partners, and indulging in more varied sexual practices, more may engage in same-sex activity. A large sample from England and Scotland had almost four in 10 teenagers (39.3%) reporting heterosexual intercourse, and 2.3% same-sex genital contact (mostly along with heterosexual intercourse) by the age of 16.[246] The effects of social influences on trends on sexual proclivities or gender identification are hardly deniable.

Recent cohorts of young adults are exposed to the media promotion of identity groups and, living amidst highly tolerant social attitudes, may be more likely to disclose sexual identity to friends and family than previous generations.[247]

Publicity also helps to grossly magnify the size of minority identity groups in the minds of the general population. It may generally be supposed that 5% of the population are transgender, although official estimates tend to put the number between 0.3% and 0.6%. The continuing influence of sexologist Alfred Kinsey is evident in the common assumption that 10% or even 15% of the population is homosexual.

To publicise and promote sexual diversity, research may expand the definition of LGB to include middle categories like 'mostly heterosexual' but 'somewhat attracted to people of your own gender'; being ever involved in 'any activities that involve physical contact and sexual arousal' with the same sex; bisexual or attracted to men and women equally; and the 'mostly homosexual' but 'somewhat attracted to people of the opposite gender'. This might deliver a more pleasing result for those content with more fluidity. One study which included those "somewhat attracted to people of your own sex" obtained a 29% 'sexual minority' of the general population.[248]

Gay journalist Matthew Parris reported in early 2021 on a UK online survey where respondents from different generations were asked about their sexual attractions. Over half (54%) of the 'Generation Z' or those under 25 years old, said they were only attracted to the opposite sex, a proportion that increased with age (84% for the 'Baby Boomers' aged 55-75). The younger the respondent, the greater the same-sex attraction, where 'mostly' attracted to the other sex and 'equally' to both sexes involved nearly a third of the youngest age group but 6% of the over 55s. The proportion saying that they were exclusively homosexually attracted remained broadly similar across all generations.

People may now not only talk more freely about the feelings they have, but "also find feelings" they didn't know they had or "feelings that can grow because a space has been created for them". The common crush on someone of the same sex during adolescence, along with intense friendships, is now sexualised. The propagation of sexual variety and experiences, in education as well as social media, may encourage people to experiment or 'explore' at ever younger ages. For "a great many people", it certainly might be that:

> ... sexuality can be channelled or re-channelled somewhat, one way or another ... poll findings lend support to this belief. That's why I've never accepted the prevailing view among gay men that "we can't help it". Some people can't. Others could. Many have. Nobody should be required to, there being nothing regrettable about being gay.[249]

Sweeping changes to the social ethos have been facilitated by the general, easy availability of contraception and abortion, together with preventatives and treatments for sexually transmitted diseases. With the complete separation of sex from procreation and largely available free from restraints, sex is simply a pleasure.

People's behaviours and attitudes owe much to what both their intimate social contacts and surrounding culture might recognise and encourage or deny and denigrate. The Add Health, a US-based nationally representative survey, has collected data across several survey waves to track changes over time, which includes the likelihood of identifying as straight for individuals who initially reported same-sex attractions and/or sexual practices or identified as something other than straight (these were offered many nuanced options). This found, perhaps unsurprisingly, that non-sexual factors like traditional values and religiosity, more than just correlated with straight sexual identification at any one point. These also predicted more moves towards a straight sexual identity for others with alternative attractions and sexual practices.[250] Those in this category were more likely to engage in SOCE therapy, which was encouraged by a belief that children should be brought up in a family with a married mother and father.

At the same time, there are the reports of the relative stability seen over time for the exclusively homosexually inclined where, in one longitudinal report on 156 gay, lesbian and bisexual youths, there were 57% who remained consistently self-identified as gay/lesbian. These scored higher in terms of certainty and self-acceptance, involvement in gay activities, being positive toward homosexuality and more comfortable with others knowing.[251] While population studies otherwise document a relatively large amount of movement away from minority sexual orientations or behaviour and attractions over the life course, this contrasts with results from samples which measure the results of therapeutic interventions. Changes here may be lower or difficult to measure (with indications that the therapeutic programmes have a rate of full identity change that peaks around 10% for participants.[252]

The fluctuations for sexualities seen in population samples may not be evidence in themselves that sexual identities and proclivities have been easily or invariably modifiable or changeable by SOCE. First, the issue is complicated by the efficacy and appropriateness of the therapies or interventions that are used, which can be amateurish or poorly informed. Secondly, those who seek therapy may also be more self-selecting because they have not made the changes to their sexual predilections that others may more easily or independently acquire or accomplish. This is something which applies to many conditions for which people seek help. This does not mean that those hoping to change in some way or to some degrees are really or secretly reluctant; nor does it imply that they are somehow resisting others' coercive pressures.

The information available does not support absolute claims about sexualities being always unchangeable, or that change attempts cause 'lasting damage'. There is yet to be a firm consensus regarding harms or benefits, or the lasting effects of reorientation therapies; outcomes might owe much to a combination of the suitability of the therapy, and the aims and commitment of the recipients. Recent research that considers more variables shows better outcomes than older studies.

Again, claims of past or prospective 'damage' should not be made unless evidence can be presented that the harm that is specific to change efforts is greater than it is for other forms of psychotherapy. Therefore: "proposals to restrict therapeutic interventions based on superficial claims of lifetime harm should be met with sceptical caution."[253]

Chapter Five

A ONE-WAY TICKET

1. The Recruiting Drive

Demands for bans on 'conversion therapy' have been sustained on a cloud of repetitious buzzwords and soundbites: 'coercive and abhorrent', 'deeply damaging', 'trauma', 'harm', etc. Politicians, not least former Prime Minister Boris Johnson, have agreed with activists in ignorance of even what is there to be addressed, apparently insensible to what the intentions of the advocates really are, and oblivious to the consequences of legislating for a ban. Here, ideas and arguments are "like rhetorical flares, sent up into the sky to awe and amaze, while distracting from the emptiness around them". [254]

What exactly a 'conversion therapy' ban is meant to cover remains ambiguous. At the same time, affirmation of what may even be transient desires has gained credence. Adults faced with a child wanting to 'transition' are encouraged to affirm what they are told. Stanton L. Jones criticised the APA for imposing incredibly high standards of success for SOCE, while having "the chutzpah to warmly recommend gay affirming therapy".[255] Activists believe that while people must not receive, or professionals provide, therapeutic help or support to move away from being gay or transgender, they can be offered a "one-way trip to the other 'gender' [or sexuality] only".[256] Thus, rather than fundamentalist religious groups, organisations like Stonewall and transgender advocates such as Mermaids might, in their affirmation of trans identity, be regarded as the exponents of a kind a 'conversion therapy'. Their perspectives are present in the Memoranda on Conversion Therapy published over recent years, which only endorse affirmation by clinicians who "acknowledge the broad spectrum of sexual orientations and gender identities and gender expressions". Although signed by 25 leading health, counselling and psychotherapy organisations, from the NHS to the Albany Trust to the Royal College of Psychiatrists to Relate, none appear to have raised questions over this 'affirmation only' policy, or the request that no sexual orientation or gender identity be regarded as "inherently preferable to any other". Both are particularly serious in terms of implications for the welfare of the young, especially with regard to the considerable promotion of sex-change options in recent years. Nor are questions asked about the relationship of these strictures to an ideology that is committed to future sexual and gender fluidity – or a culture of sex and existence without boundaries that dissolves biology itself.[257]

Together with the Coventry University researchers for the Government Equalities Office, the British Association for Counselling and Psychotherapy (BACP) favour counselling to help people relate positively to their LGBT sexual or gender identity. The Consensus Statement back in 2014 at the request of the UK Department of Health and prepared by leading psychotherapy and LGBT organisations, referred to "professionals ... specifically trained in sexual issues and, [who] therefore, have expertise in specifically helping people who are experiencing difficulties around attraction to others of the same sex."[258] It asks: "Who else can help?" and lists Stonewall and Pink Therapy.

Gillian Branstetter of the National Center for Transgender Equality in Washington, D.C. declared how "Conversion therapy is a fraudulent and dangerous practice that threatens the long-term wellbeing of LGBTQ youth everywhere it's allowed ...". Citing transgender youth facing frequent discrimination campaigns by groups that promote 'conversion therapy', she insists: "It's crucial [that] parents and healthcare providers understand that conversion therapy is a very real danger while transition-related care is safe, effective, and supported by the entire mainstream of the medical community ...". [259]

Any discomfort with or refusal to grasp and 'celebrate' the discovered or confirmed 'identity' is ascribed by activists to 'internalised homophobia' or the 'heteronormativity' that someone may have imbibed and must be addressed. In a response to a critical article, leading campaigner Jayne Ozanne explains her remit as promoting "safe spaces for LGBT+ people to explore and come to a point of peace with who they are, without being told to conform to certain stereotypes." To this end, she accepts prayer and pastoral guidance:

> ... that allows this [homosexuality] to be welcomed [while, any] prayer seeking to change or suppress an

individual's sexuality or gender identity must be banned, as it causes psychological harm, creating deep feelings of self-loathing, guilt and shame. This is the same for trans people, if not more so.[260]

Is welcoming and consolidating one identity but not another, conscription or capture? Questions about activists introducing prospective LGBT youngsters to the gay world or an alternative gender identity tend not to surface. However, if help to leave LGBT identities is forbidden 'conversion', is not affirmation of LGBT identity equally 'conversion'? Sex education or programmes like CHIPS (Combating Homophobia in Primary Schools) enthusiastically endorse sexual experimentation with the same or both sexes. Once someone moves towards LGBTQ+, there is no room for second thoughts on this one-way street. When the former UK Parliamentary Under-Secretary of State for Health drew attention in a Commons debate to the 'unintended consequences' of a ban because it "may stop counsellors practising who are supporting people coming to terms with their sexuality", this was clearly not related to going straight or avoiding transgender.[261]

Even though the government has belatedly told schools that children must not be told they were born in the wrong body, groups like Stonewall, GIRES (Gender Research & Education Society), the Proud Trust etc., have funding and blank cavasses of 'inclusivity, diversity and tolerance' for going into schools using the Sex & Relationship curriculum to promote their ideology. While guidance may claim not to "promote transitioning", this is questionable, given acquiescence to activist recommendations for teachers to 'respect' youngsters' wishes – using their preferred pronouns and recording new names for schools and local authorities.

Moving from heterosexuality to LGBTQ+ can be enthusiastically welcomed as 'coming out' to the real and better self, while the converse is dismissed or put down. A gay senior Anglican minister called upon Christians to pray for little Prince George to be gay and to be blessed one day with "the love of a fine young gentleman".[262] This resulted in nothing of the kind of furore that would have erupted had he prayed for little George to be heterosexual. In former times, a person's "odd gay kiss or more" might have been "the aberration – the falling away from the norm" but now, for Douglas Murray, "the culture suggests that the gay kiss is the moment of revelatory truth".[263]

When it becomes imperative to embrace and 'celebrate' LGBT identity as the true, intrinsic self-identity, retraction is not an option. Progression is only in one direction, as the "perception has developed that to once be gay is to have fallen into your true state of nature, whereas to be forever afterwards straight is not", and similarly for gender change.[264] Councillor Gareth Roberts, leader of Richmond upon Thames council, which painted the zebra crossings with LGBTQ+ colours, stands with "residents to combat the intolerance of homophobia, biphobia and transphobia" and then asks, "is simply being tolerant quite what we should be aiming for?" He recounts how, at a conference:

> A young trans activist took to the stage and made a simple point; their opening line was "I'm transgender

and I don't want to be tolerated." Well, it was enough to grab the attention and from thereon in [as] they expanded on their message. To be tolerated is to be put up with, it's to be grudgingly accepted. Who wants that? What they wanted was to be celebrated. They were right, the rich diversity in our communities and beyond – a diversity which is all too easy to take for granted – is something which we should all celebrate. It was a simple yet powerfully made point and one which I'd never really considered before, because being tolerant is a good thing isn't it?[265]

Respect is one thing, but why do trans youngsters need to be 'celebrated'? What do they do or represent to merit such acclaim? Who else might want to be 'celebrated'? For what should anyone be 'celebrated'? Who chooses? Should some be able to command all others to celebrate them? Why are some meant to have a privileged status absent for others, who are then obliged to 'celebrate' them?

Overridden are considerations of the volatility and fluidity of adolescent and early adulthood attractions and behaviour. The frequently effervescent quality of gender shifts should suggest greater caution when it comes to affirmation, particularly where this can involve bodily reconstruction. With adolescence being a confusing time, neural mechanisms can lead to heightened responsiveness to reward emotional cues, although capacities for behavioural and emotional regulation are still comparatively immature.[266] Might affirming a youngster as a different sex or sexual identity in front of their peers and seniors amount to entrapment? A later wish to move out of how someone may have been earlier defined, may involve having to deal with those around them whom they feel they might have misled. Is unquestioning affirmation and 'celebration' a form of "conversion therapy"? With schools primed to be on the lookout for budding LGBTQs, these may be youngsters who experience any same-sex attraction, attribution, contact or curiosity, or who have been the target of 'homophobic' or 'transphobic' bullying. A report circulates of parents receiving a letter informing them that they and their six-year-old son would be deemed transphobic, unless he affirmed that another boy in class was now a girl.

There are serious questions here as to whether there should be any encouragement or pressure on youngsters to fix upon any 'identity'. Interventions to validate or affirm 'gay' or transgender youngsters early in life may not only be misplaced but may expose them to problems which could otherwise be avoided. There are, not least, concerns that those children who are allowed or encouraged to transition to the opposite gender may later regret the change and seek to return to their 'assigned' birth sex.

To counter such anxieties, a recent US study is proclaimed to strongly refute "suggestions by politicians and others that those who seek medical care have a high rate of regret or retransition". To examine retransition rates for early transitioning children, 317 socially transitioned 'transgender' children participated [sic] in the longitudinal Trans Youth Project (TYP) between 2013 and 2017. Of these, 124 began transitioning before six years of age and 193 at six years or older (the average age was 8). The participants had to have made a 'binary social transition' which principally related to changing their pronouns although, at entry, 37 had already begun puberty blockers. Five years later, there are claims by M. Brett Cooper, MD, of UT Southwestern Medical Center, Dallas, of "evidence to support that persistent, insistent, and consistent youth" who "identify as transgender early and are supported through a social transition have an extremely low rate of retransition to a gender that aligns with their sex assigned at birth". Only 7.3% of the participants had purportedly retransitioned.

The study used a volunteer sample, which cannot be generalised to the population at large and has an enormous potential for bias. There was no evaluation whether the participants met the DSM-5 criteria for childhood gender dysphoria, only that, based "on data collected at their [researchers] initial visit", they showed signs of gender identification and preferences at odds with those "commonly associated" with "sex assigned at birth ...". This, like the assessment at follow-up, centred on the use of cross-sex pronouns. The parents might have strongly endorsed and reinforced the cross-sex identification of these young children. Was their enthusiastic support the reason why they enrolled them in this programme in the first place?[267]

It has been mentioned how the focus on banning spiritual variants of 'conversion therapy' easily stretches to encompass teaching or preaching on traditional sexual ethics, embodied in common assumptions or understandings about sexuality and gender. These beliefs clash with those of activists, who may be not so much committed to civil rights or equality or safety, but to "a desire to reshape the views and ideals and habits of the public, to enforce a new morality ...".[268] After all, there no law that applies to a heterosexual that does not apply to a homosexual, or a right that they do not have. This is no longer about rights, supporting LGBT pupils, or even ridding society of its Christian underpinnings, but involves a new:

> ... framework carved out by those who apparently know better than us what our private lives and relationships should and shouldn't look like ... you're a moral heretic whose very thoughts and behaviour are seen as deviant, as running counter to a new, apparently better kind of morality. And that ... simply will not be tolerated.

Such plans for a social and moral overhaul have arisen while the traditional or conjugal family has been undefended, if not under concerted attack. A "sacralisation" of sexual and gender variations:

> ... corresponds precisely with the growing denigration by the state and others of the sphere of the family and the ideals of lifelong commitment, because celebrating gayness has become the main and most PC means through which traditional values might be dented and traditional identities called into question ...[269]

This witnesses to how the cultural downgrading of 'heteronormativity' plays out. Heteronormativity describes how social institutions and policies reinforce the presumption that people are heterosexual, and that gender and sex are natural binaries. Critics argue that this is all oppressive, stigmatising, and marginalises perceived 'deviant' forms of sexuality and gender, making self-expression difficult when this does not conform to the norm. The answer for 'queer' theory ideologists is the dissolution of all categories, so that all can then take up sexualities and bodily forms throughout life much at will.[270] All then, for Peter Tatchell, becomes "… a choice, and we should be glad it's that way and celebrate it for ourselves".[271]

The comprehensive purging of heteronormativity opens onto relationships freed from structure, normative guidance and standards, where there is a kaleidoscope of ever-diversifying relations and sexual experiences, with the end of the very idea – and existence – of male and female. This is epitomised by *Educate and Celebrate* run by Elly Barnes, MBE (for her contribution to equality, education and diversity). With links to the Socialist Workers Party, she uses art and music lessons to help "embed gender, gender identity and sexual orientation into the fabric" of schools. Her bottom line is to "completely smash heteronormativity" and make curricula, teachers and pupils 'gender neutral'. This social reconfiguration, which is in accord with tenets of the earlier sexual revolution, proceeds under the banner of 'tolerance' and 'diversity'.

If activists can abolish the influence that one generation has over the next, their hoped-for future can emerge without obstruction. Then, in the fluid void, "we no longer ask 'boy or girl' in order to start gendering an infant … only then will men and women be socially interchangeable and really equal."[272] The pansexual, genderqueer, or non-binary self is untethered from any biological facts and can be constantly redefined and reshaped. In this new society, gender is the way in which a person feels about themselves, irrespective of their sex organs or the 'sex' they were given at birth.

As the liberated world is one of omnisexuality (LGBTQQIP2SAA: lesbian, gay, bisexual, transgender, questioning, queer, intersex, pansexual, two-spirit, androgynous and asexual) so, in recognition and preparation, there must be diverse, non-heteronormative environments in nursery, primary school, senior school and university or college. At first, this looks akin to further pigeon-holing everyone into an ever-increasing number of boxes, where they must stay ever after. However, when heterosexuality becomes the moribund outsider, this almost solves the activist's dilemma; paradoxically, fluidity is reconciled with the solidity of a wide variety of non-heterosexual sexual and gender identities in a polymorphous blend.

Schools have been ensuring that lessons and activities reflect, advance and celebrate the range of sexual and gender identities, with LGBT campaign groups listed by the DfE as leading sources of educational resources.[273] Schools might be downgraded by Ofsted for not being sufficiently LGBT, even with the best pastoral care (as for Kingham Hill in Oxfordshire). Parents tell of a five-year-old coming home relating how their teacher says a boy could choose to be a girl if he wanted to, or of their child's bemusement at a boy parading in a frilly dress, with teachers at primary schools using assemblies to explain that a certain boy would return as a girl, or *vice versa*, the following day.[274]

The BBC is advised to use children's programming to positively "familiarise audiences through incidental portrayal from an early age" with homo/bi-sexuality and family variations along with the validation of children who are homo/bisexual.[275] By 2018, it was running *Just a Girl* – a programme for children aged 6 to 12 – illustrating how someone may be born into the 'wrong body' and could take hormone blockers to halt the physical changes puberty portends. Along with now numerous programmes about 'trans kids', drag queens or queer role models perform for children in libraries, schools and bookstores, with gender fluidity in the form of men dressed up as grotesque parodies of women, often portrayed in performances with highly sexualised language.

Elaborating in a guide for primary pupils aged three and over, Stonewall speaks of how "babies are labelled as a boy or a girl. When some people get older, they realise that the label they were given was wrong." *Who Are You? The Kid's Guide to Gender Identity*, tells how people only 'guess' a baby's sex and offers a multiplicity of identities they might prefer, such as 'genderqueer, non-binary, bigender, neutrois (neutral or void) and two-spirit'.[276] Teachers, school managers, administrators and others are themselves likely to be in receipt of training and instruction on imparting radical sexual ideologies to pupils. Proselytisation is prioritised. *Supporting Transgender Pupils in Schools – Guidance for Scottish Schools* (informed by LGBT Youth Scotland) – effectively tells teachers that trans 'rights' supersede those of everybody else. As in other promotional educational material, heterosexual and natal gender pupils are side-lined, while transgender pupils must inhabit all-encompassing affirmative environments, with teaching materials featuring transgender people. Rather than question youngsters with gender identity issues, teachers are told to ask simply what name they would like to be known by and which toilet they would like to use.

They may be assured that their information will not be shared, even with parents, while the schools work to "correct" those unsupportive and labouring under "misconceptions". This "getting it right for every child approach", is being "inclusive of and responsive to transgender identities, even if there are no 'out' transgender young people in the school".[277] In their absence, this identity is an ideal for pupils to admire.

Is this grooming and is it "conversion" to an ideology which permits no disagreement in any form? Challenging it has meant people ending up in court, deluged with death threats, and with speakers cancelled or de-platformed. A US senator was jeered when she said: "even fundamental scientific truths, such as the existence of two sexes, male and female, are subject to challenge these days ...", even though she clarified: "I am not making a comment on the fact that there are people who transition between sexes". She would later apologise. [278]

Conflict over conversion therapy has recently become more than simply a matter of LGBT+ versus heteronormality. In 2021, Lord Herbert of South Downs (a Tory peer) was drawing attention to how the "worst current form of conversion therapy" is where young gay and lesbian people were being influenced that they should be transgender.[279] Some LGB activists, particularly lesbians, are speaking of a new brand of "conversion" therapy, which is also blamed on 'heteronormativity' – something which purportedly drives gays and lesbians to change their sex, although Peter Tatchell sees sex-change as a way to evade one form of prejudice by embracing an identity that attracts even more.[280]

It may well be that a young female with male inclinations could be an old-fashioned lesbian, rather than a modern transgender person. How often does this apply to those seeking transitioning, with claims now being repeated *ad nauseam* that transgender-interested youngsters are more or less *ipso facto* 'gay'? "Since most are same-sex attracted, does hasty gender transition amount to 'converting' gay kids?" asks Janice Turner in *The Times*.[281]

There is a study of 77 US youngsters aged 5-12 years who had been referred to clinics because of gender dysphoria, and followed up at 16-28 years (23 were untraceable). Over a quarter (27%) of respondents were persistently gender dysphoric, extremely cross-gendered in behaviour and feelings, and homosexual or bisexual. In the gender dysphoric desistence group (43%) all the girls and half of the boys reported being heterosexual.[282]

For activist groups such as Stonewall and Mermaids, even a temporary incongruent identity taken up by an adolescent can be their 'true self' or 'innate being', that must receive endorsement. This century has seen a massive increase in referrals of children to the NHS's GIDS (Gender Identity Services) clinic, approaching 5,000% over the last ten years. The numbers were 2,590 in 2018-19, or more than triple the referrals a few years before in 2014-15, and included ten for 3 and 4-year-olds,

21 for 5-year-olds, and 43 for 9-year-olds. One half of those with gender identity development problems in 2020 were under 14, with girls representing three-quarters (76%) of those who wanted gender change compared with around 50% less than a decade earlier. A fact-check showed that the average number of children referred to GIDS each week grew from two in 2009-2010 to 50 in 2017-2019. The sharp rise after 2015-2016 might coincide with the media's launch of high-profile transgender celebs as part of a promotional tide.[283]

The surge in numbers might be ascribed to how "kids just feel safer identifying as trans now that there is greater awareness and acceptance in society ...", as much as LGB children are now safer 'coming out'.[284] They are said to be 'safer' when, at the same time, they are portrayed as persecuted in a transphobic and homophobic heteronormative society. The explanation given varies according to the context.

The 'affirmation' route has meant puberty blockers from around 10 years of age and cross-sex hormones from 16. The NHS might maintain that only youngsters who show lasting signs of gender dysphoria and meet strict criteria should be referred to a hormone specialist for puberty blockers. They must be aged 16 or over and have been on puberty blockers for at least 12 months before they can proceed to cross-sex hormones. Activists and critics alike claim it is quicker to get a gender dysphoria diagnosis and hormone blockers than to access psychiatric help.[285]

Although surgical bodily reconstruction is not meant to take place until 18, many girls under this age use breast-binders or have their breasts removed ('top surgery' or double mastectomy), which happens before there is much chance to reflect on the implications. Hormone pills and breast binders may be available online if these cannot be obtained on the NHS or even from private clinics. Girls on hormones can expect facial hair, deepened voice, baldness, sterility, and vaginal atrophy. There are insufficiently explored suggestions of elevated risks of, not least, osteoporosis, mood disorders, and cognitive impairment, together with increased risks for heart attacks, blood clots and cancers.[286] Non-operative interventions like breast-binding or penis/scrotum tucking have their own negative health impacts. There are risks for functionality or even satisfaction. While flesh may be removed from the arm to make a (non-operative) penis, the reality is that fully functioning female sex and reproductive organs cannot be replaced with male sex and reproductive organs, or *vice versa*. At most, this is cosmetic surgery. In an extraordinary and alarming paradox, therapeutic support that mutilates and amputates body parts to "transition" may not be considered to be 'conversion therapy', but talking therapy is.

Approved 'affirmation' may be creating serious problems that have been largely disregarded. There has been little questioning or investigation – probably because of professional bans – about why so many youngsters have become uncomfortable with the body that they were born in and desire to become the opposite sex. Cases have accumulated, particularly for females, alleging that their problems were not clinically addressed before they went down the transition route. In 2019, a Detransition

Advocacy Network was launched by women, often minus wombs, ovaries and breasts. This has been met with a response that blames any withdrawal from a trans identity on an unsupportive and hostile transphobic environment.[287]

Must claims of an incongruent gender identity be treated as the innate or 'true self', however enthusiastic the youngster is for a change? Sven Román, a Swedish specialist in child and adolescent psychiatry explains that, while affirmative responses mean "drastic treatment with high doses of sex hormones and breast and genital surgery", this is "despite the lack of any scientific evidence for these treatments for children, and probably not for young adults either."[288] (Stockholm saw an eight-to-ten-fold increase in referrals to gender dysphoria reception centres for children in three years.) As much as youngsters have fantastical beliefs about reality, how much do those pursuing gender change have any real ideas of what this involves, especially in the long term? How much is suggested by media, educational campaigns, and public displays, or spread through online chat rooms as much as in classrooms and playgrounds? With social contagion, which girls are more prone to, people will believe almost anything to fit in with the group.

Pupils who are convinced that they are transgender may persuade others to join – with grooming online or from 'support groups' which operate like cults with clubs and internet chat rooms. In nearly 37% of the friendship groups described in a prominent US study, most of the members became transgender-identified. As these adolescent and young adult children 'came out', their mental well-being and parent-child relationships worsened. As they might try and isolate themselves from their families, they were also likely to express distrust of non-transgender people and stop spending time with non-transgender friends.[289] There might be similar encouragement from LGBT clubs in schools and further educational establishments, run by external identity groups; once a youngster is persuaded to participate, it may be difficult to withdraw or reject a gay or trans-sexual identity.

Those with autistic traits and perhaps comorbidities involving anxiety and depression might be particularly susceptible. There are claims that:

> … at least 75 percent of patients with gender dysphoria have other psychiatric problems. In the group of children and young adults, autism, eating disorders, self-harm behaviour and abuse are common. For all these conditions there is evidence-based treatment. Given such, gender dysphoria often disappears, as it is usually secondary to these conditions.[290]

High levels of autistic traits have been repeatedly identified for youngsters with gender identity disorder (GID)/Gender Disorder (GD) and especially for female to male subjects (this does not mean that transgenderism itself is a symptom of autism).[291] In recent research, 14% in a sample of 177 transgender and non-binary individuals had a diagnosis of autistic spectrum disorder (compared with 4% for 'cisgenders') and a further 28% reached the cut-off point or margin for diagnosis, compared with none for the 'cisgenders'. This was primarily driven by high scoring amongst those 'assigned' female at birth (trans men).[292] A Dutch sample of young people with gender dysphoria similarly had high co-occurring autistic traits relative to the general population.[293]

A study across the Netherlands, Belgium, Germany and Norway, found that almost 70% of the transsexual participants also showed one or more Axis I disorders (mental health and substance abuse disorders), with 27% currently the most affected, whilst 17% had anxiety disorders. Figures were respectively, 60% and 28% over lifetime. With some variation across countries, these were higher than for general populations.[294]

A study over two years of Finnish gender dysphoric adolescent applicants (mean age 16 and mostly girls) for sex reassignment found that autism spectrum disorders (ASD) exceeded the prevalence for the general population by almost three-fold. Seventy-five per cent of the applicants for reassignment had been, or were currently undergoing, child and adolescent psychiatric treatment for reasons other than gender dysphoria. These were: depression; anxiety disorders; suicidal and self-harming behaviours; psychotic symptoms; conduct disorders; substance abuse; autism spectrum disorder; and ADHD. There was social isolation and bullying, which was unrelated to gender dysphoria or incongruence. The researchers speak of gender dysphoria presenting in the "context of wider identity confusion, severe psychopathology and considerable challenges in the adolescent development."[295] Affirming transition for children in these circumstances amounts to mutilating and sterilizing emotionally troubled youth.[296]

Others who recognise that "transgender and non-binary (TNB) youths are disproportionately burdened by poor mental health outcomes including depression, anxiety and suicidal ideation and attempts" see these "disparities" as "likely owing to high levels of social rejection, such as a lack of support from parents and bullying." [297] This is unlikely.

With the incidence of comorbidity now well established for transgender and gender-diverse individuals, in one recent large-scale study these had higher rates of autism, along with elevated rates of six other neurodevelopmental and psychiatric conditions, compared with 'cisgender' individuals. The highest effect size was for schizophrenia.[298] Autism spectrum disorders are neurodevelopmental disorders which affect social communication and understanding. These are distinct from schizophrenia but overlap somewhat with this where, not least, they share abnormalities in prenatal development.[299] Those with autistic traits or predispositions have fixations and persevere intensely with behaviours or objectives acquired virtually at random. With sex-change being much publicised and endorsed, they may more likely be convinced that they are the wrong sex and obsessively focus on pharmacological and surgical transition.

Munchausen syndrome by proxy may operate where a parent insists on bringing up a boy as a girl or *vice versa*. When parents are caught up with transgender ideology and refuse to reveal their baby's sex, this might facilitate a virtually arbitrary imposition of one or the other on a child. This could be encouraged where, for example, NHS trusts endorse guidance (Supporting Trans People), which declared that "anatomy is not always a good guide to what gender a child will be or even what sex they are" and emphasised how doing nothing or delaying treatment causes harm.[300] Results from a 20-year Swedish longitudinal cohort study show persistently high levels of psychiatric illness many years after medical transition. [301]

Might not children need to undergo puberty to know whether they are misplaced in their bodies? Those blocked from experiencing puberty overwhelmingly go on to take cross-sex hormones (oestrogen for boys or testosterone for girls) as the prelude to physical reassignment. Of 70 adolescents who received puberty suppression between 2000 and 2008, none withdrew, and all began cross-sex hormone treatment.[302] Most who take and then abandon blockers do not experience a delayed or any puberty, which undermines claims that the effects are easily reversed. Along with the effects on bone and brain development, there is the prospect of infertility. Without this treatment, the vast majority of children with gender incongruence will outgrow this if puberty takes a natural course, with estimates for desisters ranging from 70% to 98% for boys and 50% to 88% for girls.[303] The period between 10 and 13 years of age may be crucial.[304] That most confused children will revert to an identity congruent with their birth sex might not be relayed to patients, parents, teachers or the public. Nor is how a pre-pubertal child cannot properly understand side-effects such as a lack of adult sex function or fertility.

With an effective professional ban on psychiatric evaluation and counselling, clinicians dealing with the gender confused may not have dared to question self-identification out of fear of accusations. As mentioned, there has been considerable pressure on professionals in medical including psychiatric settings to comply with identity group perspectives.[305]

Results such as the politicisation of medical issues hinder research, which further harms those with gender dysphoria. Fertility expert Lord (Robert) Winston speaks about how his clinic has been seeing "the long-term results for often very unhappy people".

Perhaps:

> One has to consider when you're doing any kind of medicine where you're trying to do good not harm, and looking at the long-term effects of what you might be doing ... [306]

In 2020, systematic reviews, spurred on by mounting evidence of psychiatric comorbidities, were concluding that clinical practice guidelines, like those provided by the World Professional Association for Transgender Health Standards of Care, were based on weak evidence.[307] One commissioned in the UK by the National Health Service described the evidence for puberty blockers and cross-sex hormones to be of 'very low certainty'.[308] It had not been taken into consideration how the youngsters now presenting with dysphoria were a radically different and little understood cohort from those previously approved for cross-sex hormones and surgery.

Along with mental health issues, there are tragic accounts of detransitioners speaking of how therapists "only knew how to encourage transitioning and reinforced the harmful ideas that led to my wrongly identifying as [female-to-male] in the first place.[309] To powerful identity groups, it might be reaffirming natal sex and privileging heteronormativity when a therapist explores a girl's claims of 'feeling like a boy'.

All adds to rising international unease over whether politics should determine how medicine is practised, particularly where this involves irreversible interventions on vulnerable populations which are, increasingly (and belatedly) realised to be unsupported by evidence. Leading Swedish psychiatrist Christopher Gillberg has said that facilitating early transition is "possibly one of the greatest scandals in medical history", with calls for an immediate ban on the use of puberty blocker drugs because of their little understood long-term effects. Finland and Sweden have curtailed or stopped youth sex transitions or prohibited gender affirming care (GAC), citing safety, efficacy, and ethical issues. Sex transition can only proceed under strict protocols, in recognition of its experimental nature. [310]

In April 2021, Arkansas passed Act 626, or the Arkansas Save Adolescents from Experimentation (SAFE) Act – becoming the first state to outlaw GAC for youth, which others might follow. In March 2022, Florida's Parental Rights in Education bill came into law, forbidding the inclusion of lessons on sexual orientation and gender identity to the curriculum for children aged 4 to 8. The LGBT group Equality Florida threatens legal action if this "endangers a single child, silences a single teacher or negatively impacts a single family". Critics dubbed it the 'Don't say Gay' law, while President Biden called it "hateful" and one senator envisaged "hundreds of kids standing outside screaming for their rights".[311]

Activists talk of how "coordinated attacks against lesbian, gay, bisexual, transgender, and queer (LGBTQ) rights have escalated in an unprecedented fashion", ranging from banning sports participation to these "most recent attacks on transgender youths and their bodies".[312] They describe a 'desistence myth', designed to 'torment' trans kids, which argues that desisting youngsters are not truly trans to begin with. But are all those who take puberty blockers real 'trans kids'?

The UK is still more in line with those jurisdictions where anyone (parent, therapist or teacher) who queries or wants to examine why a youngster insists that they are in the wrong body, is construed as using "conversion therapy". A particular concern relates to whether a comprehensive ban, with threats of prosecution, will prevent youngsters affected by educational or media materials from receiving anything but affirmative directives for sex-change. Could parent-child conversations result in police enquiries, particularly where obedient teachers and mischievous youngsters pass on information?

A report of the Care Quality Commission (CQC) into the Gender Identity Service (GIDS) at the Tavistock and Portman NHS clinic noted failures to assess the competency and capacity of young people treated for gender dysphoria, along with poor record keeping, a disregard for staff who "said they felt unable to raise concerns without fear of retribution" and pressure on parents to approve their children's reassignment.[313] The following interim report from Dr Hilary Cass's Review for NHS England in 2022, on clinical practice for children and young people, would flag up how there was a lack of open discussion about gender dysphoria and a clinical approach that was not "subjected to some of the normal quality controls". This adopted "predominantly an affirmative, non-exploratory approach, often driven by child and parent expectations", with no consistent processes in place to identify the vulnerable.[314]

Rather than the further moves against discussion which are threatened by bans on 'conversion therapy', there should perhaps be mandatory investigation and counselling before anyone embarks on sex changes. In place of accepting youngsters' claims that they were born the wrong body, examination of the possible reasons for gender dysphoria and transition demands should cover mental health and investigation of the prevalence of co-morbid disorders, along with discussion of options and consequences. Otherwise, there is an abdication of adult responsibility as child protection is "sacrificed to a political and ideological stance".[315] Some, like Keira Bell, who have challenged the rules that allowed their early transition and later regretted the change, doubt that there could be any help for people in her position if a legal conversion ban were enacted.

Yet, as these serious concerns are raised so, in the first scheme in the UK and backed by Stonewall, family doctors are being offered payment for prescribing to transgender patients. Beginning in Sussex, GPs will get

£178 a year for every adult to whom they prescribe "cross sex hormone therapy" or testosterone to help with masculinisation for trans men, and oestrogen to help with feminisation, and be able to claim an extra £91 for providing annual health checks to transgender, non-binary or intersex (TNBI) patients. Alongside improving access to hormones, the scheme requires staff to take training in transgender healthcare. This purportedly aims to reduce the high rates of long-term physical and mental health problems of patients together with the burgeoning gender clinic waiting lists. With any decision to start hormone therapy "at the discretion of the individual GP", this raises further issues of access by those under-age, and possible encouragement for the transgender surge.

2. Where Are We Going from Here?

The call to ban "conversion therapy" was launched amid tales of 'coercive and abhorrent' electrocutions and rapes. Might attention not better focus on how the state itself is sanctioning and enabling experimentation on youngsters. There is a law against FGM (female genital mutilation), then why not one against the removal of healthy organs and other body parts? Professional restrictions on openly discussing matters relating to gender change with clients should end even if, for some trans-identifying patients, hormones and operations may be the best course. People need to talk about their anxieties. Instead of driving help underground, whether for problems involving either sexuality or transgenderism, it would be better to have informed, accredited therapists who can provide services. There also needs to be systematic interdisciplinary and impartial investigative research free from the influence or control of identity factions and distinct from matters of discrimination. Proper empirical examination cannot be carried out without freedom to investigate, think and discuss.

Stonewall's influence in the EHRC (Equality and Human Rights Commission) waned after chairman Lady Falkner of Margravine replaced David Isaac (who then became Master of Worcester College Oxford) and the EHRC withdrew from Stonewall's Diversity Champions programme. Noting public concern over the conflict between trans and women's rights, there was some defence for the right to hold "gender critical beliefs" without abuse and job loss. Now that the EHRC is raising valid concerns instead of being completely in step with Stonewall, critics are labelling it 'political'. Perhaps everything is political where there is a necessity to engage in debate.

Aware that the criminalisation of 'conversion therapy' would impede investigation of gender dysphoria and related developmental problems, the EHRC said that prohibition on trans conversion should wait until the completion of the review on NHS gender identity services.[316] It now emphasised how special "consideration" should be given to "whether a differentiated approach" was needed "to what constitutes conversion therapy in relation to sexual orientation and being transgender". Again, "legislation must define clearly what is meant by sexual orientation and being transgender". Should the Government decide to proceed with proposals to ban both types of "harmful conversion therapy practices", a "draft Bill should be published for pre-legislative scrutiny by a Committee of both Houses of Parliament" which "contains clear definitions and terminology so that its effects can be properly understood and is evidence-based and proportionate".

In consideration for religion, it emphasised that "LGBT people" should not:

> ... be prevented from seeking spiritual support from their faith leader in the exploration of their sexual orientation or being transgender, including within their families, schools and communities. Encouraging people to comply with religious doctrine that requires refraining from certain types of sexual activity should not fall within the definition of conversion therapy either.

However, this goes with the warning that "community leaders should be made aware of the ban on conversion therapy in order that they understand the importance of compliance".

After Boris Johnson's administration dropped the prospect of a ban, and then quickly re-instated it, the Queen's speech on 10th May 2022 promised that legislation "will be introduced to ban conversion therapy". Reflecting the latest EHRC perspectives, this would initially apply only to sexual orientation, not to transgender. There was said to be not enough information available to proceed on trans conversion therapy, which would be dealt with as more becomes available. Under 18s would be unable to consent to any procedure under any circumstances while, with strict controls, adults could consent to measures for 'exploring their sexuality'. Many Tory MPs including former Prime Minister Theresa May were disappointed, particularly about the transgender exclusion.[317] PinkNews reported how the proposals "shuddered rage through not only the queer community but the government itself, with one of its top LGBTQ+ advisors quitting in protest." The adviser referred to was Iain Anderson, proclaimed as the country's first 'LGBT+ business champion' tasked with driving equality in the workplace.[318] The British Association for Counselling and Psychotherapy was "shocked and disappointed".[319] A spokesperson for trans youth charity Mermaids reportedly claimed that the exclusion of "trans and non-binary people from the ban … is sending an extremely dangerous message to the wider public that our systematic persecution is acceptable and is securing decades more harm to be perpetrated against trans people." What is this "systematic persecution"? [320] Allowing anyone with transgender issues to consent to treatment for reversing a sexual transitioning would, according to Jayne Ozanne, continue to put "many lives at risk".

As if in conciliation, the EHRC insisted that 'uncontroversial proposals' to ban therapy designed to 'make gay people straight' should be brought in as soon as possible, along with more money to tackle LGBT bullying in schools. While stressing that this would not prevent priests and other religious leaders advising congregations on sexual matters, questions remain about when this strays into 'conversion therapy'. Stonewall and others are not to be appeased over the omission of trans-gender 'conversion therapy' from the proposed ban.

Coincidentally, plans for the *'Safe to be Me'* conference scheduled for June 2022 disintegrated, boycotted by most of those expected to attend. The advance of £8m or more of public money may have to be written off. According to the *Times* newspaper, this was *Undone by Intolerance*; but whose intolerance? Ironically, Stonewall's prioritisation of the transgender agenda over gay rights had increased estrangement between LGBT factions which have become increasingly riven by ideological disputes and recriminations. But why go in the first place, and for what? Aside from the disputes over whose cause has precedence, the observation that the Government "was hopelessly muddled" here, and "seemed to have little idea what the conference would do or who should attend" might apply to the whole "conversion therapy" saga.[321]

Policy by soundbite or buzzword provides phantoms to chase, when the 'coercive and abhorrent' bubble would have been better pricked from the start. All illustrates how easy it is to insist that something be made illegal, even in the absence of precisely what it is supposedly meant to cover. Claims about electrocution have receded, although there are still assertions that, for example, conversion therapy "can, in extreme forms, include physical violence and torturous practices". According to a *Daily Mail* writer, the "UN has said the practice amounts to torture and should be outlawed".[322]

As poorly defined and amorphous causes offer an enormous blank canvas to fill, with little guidance as to where any line might be drawn, some have sensed opportunities to abolish religion or, certainly, Christian practice. Throughout any examination of demands for bans, it is hard to avoid how it is moral and religious perspectives that are primary targets. There are accusations that these motivate or coerce individuals to pursue 'conversion therapy' and use oppressive or outright violent procedures. Hence, everyday religious activities, ranging from prayers to teachings on sexual ethics and pastoral consultations, must be outlawed for bringing 'direct harm' to LGBT people.

The prospective ban on variants of change therapy is a denial of individual freedom and choice which will, along with more intervention in schools, further consolidate the controls exercised by activist identity groups. These lobbies should have no power or influence at all over policies and procedures which should be based on knowledge, general ethical understandings and equal consideration for all.

Proposals for "conversion therapy" bans have been part of the accelerating grip of censorship and intolerance throughout society. Together with the increasing restrictions on free speech, these proposals continue to trend into ever more alarming suggestions. Picking up on the Government's original proposals for the ban, Charlotte Nichols, Labour MP for Warrington North, insists on Protection Orders for those undergoing or deemed 'at risk' of "conversion therapy". It is envisaged that such orders for those thought 'vulnerable' to cultural or religious pressure to suppress, deny or forcibly change their sexuality or gender identity will make it simpler for statutory support services to help such people 'in need'. This would come with 'multi-agency risk assessment conferences' for these 'safeguarded' individuals. If deemed to be at risk, will they be restrained? Arrested? Monitored? Under house arrest? Imprisoned? Sectioned (detained) under mental health legislation? What is the degree of coercion or influence that might prompt official involvement? Will this encourage vigilantes seeking miscreants to monitor? Would these raid churches and restrain people who may be voluntarily seeking prayer for something they want to leave?

Then there is the move to apply the language of the Prevent Duty (designed to identify potential terrorists), which could mean that any remaining counselling services would be liable to being reported for extremism. How might 'cultural and religious pressure' be defined, if a particular church might be the only place to go for help when therapists and counsellors are under professional and legal bans? Would a 'detransitioner' be on the wrong side of the law, along with anyone who helps them?

Even what is commonly proposed may affect social workers, counsellors, clerics, doctors, and teachers or anyone who might want to understand 'why' a child presents with gender dysphoria. Could a parent who complains that their child has been unduly influenced by LGBT ideology at school, or caught up on a media fad, be accused of 'suppressing' their 'true identity'? Perhaps a girl says, "Mummy, maybe I'm a boy" after hearing that sex is for choosing. Is it 'conversion therapy' and 'transphobic' to say: "You will grow out of it" or "If you have a vagina, you are a girl"? To Stonewall or Mermaids, it might well be. There are those who may not want their daughter to have her breasts cut off, grow a beard, or their son castrated. This is likely to be more out of loving concern than tyrannous control.

There are parallels with recent moves on 'hate speech' where there was a proposal (rejected for England but applied in Scotland) to criminalise speech in private dwellings. According to Alicia Kearns MP, there must be a legal requirement to report known or suspected cases of 'conversion' therapy – the kind of reporting that is associated with despotic regimes. This might cause animosity and trouble between neighbours, workers and acquaintances if malicious or mistaken, or any, accusations are made. What could instigate complaints: an overheard private conversation between parents and children? An aspiration of the Scottish Parliament is for a "distinct reporting mechanism for children" to presumably be able report their parents or others for not appropriately affirming their present choice of identity. The freedom to discuss matters of sexuality and gender and surrounding issues needs to be protected.

Linking therapy to torture might aim to ensure that proposed bans cannot possibly be contested. However, allegations that so-called 'conversion therapy' "can cause long lasting damage to those who go through it" is not borne out by evidence.[323] The clearly established 'long lasting damage' is to youth from gender reassignment measures. If the fantasies about thousands irrevocably 'damaged' by brutal zealots can be left behind, attention should turn to removing a "toxic ideology out of the

NHS, schools, libraries, charities, BBC, police, prisons, our political parties".[324]

Legislation should never be pushed through without consideration of what exactly it intends to cover and achieve. Idealistic notions of saving people from coercion are, as elsewhere, often a cloak for totalitarian and oppressive measures that are a precursor to the oversight and management of people's lives. The authoritarian demands of strident minorities should not be enshrined in law. People should have rights to self-determination and be free to make their own life choices, including being able to move away from whatever they do not want and seek help to do so. To deny this is no more inclusive than it is ethical.

The proposed prohibitions are serious threats to freedom of choice and speech. They have wide-ranging potential for considerable interference in many aspects of personal and social life, including the welfare of children and vulnerable adults who are put at the risk of exploitation and life-changing injuries to appease ideological aspirations. Based upon the evidence, any ban on so called 'conversion therapy' must be rejected.

NOTES

1 https://www.gov.uk/government/consultations/banning-conversion-therapy
2 Memorandum of Understanding on Conversion Therapy in the UK, Version 2, Update March 2022
3 Following the Queen's Speech on Tuesday, 11.05.2021, former Minister for Women and Equalities, Liz Truss, confirmed that the government would take legislative steps to ban "conversion therapy". Equality Hub, Government Equalities Office, and The Rt Hon Elizabeth Truss MP 11.05.2021 and 'Banning Conversion Therapy', Presented to Parliament op. cit.
4 Clarke, S. et al., *Lesbian, Gay, Bisexual, Trans and Queer Psychology,* Cambridge University Press, 2010
5 Geraint Davies, 14.01.2014, Column 706, *Hansard*, House of Commons
6 United Nations, 'Ending violence and discrimination against lesbian, gay, bisexual, transgender and intersex people', Joint statement, September 2015
7 Ibid.
8 'Banning Conversion Therapy', Presented to Parliament by the Secretary of State, op. cit.
9 Report on petition PE1817, 'End conversion therapy', Equalities, Human Rights and Civil Justice Committee, Scottish Parliament, 25.01.2022
10 Ibid.
11 Mental health support if you're lesbian, gay, bisexual or trans (LGBTQ+) 02.07.2020. NHS
12 LGBTQ+ Action Plan | GOV.WALES https://gov.wales › lgbtq-action-plan
13 Conversion Therapy – Victim Support Service, Crown Commercial Service, 22.12.2021
14 Ryan, C. et al., 'Parent-initiated sexual orientation change efforts with LGBT adolescents: Implications for young adult mental

health and adjustment', *Journal of Homosexuality,* 2018 67(2), 159-173

[15] 'UN expert calls for global ban on practices of so-called "conversion therapy"', *United Nations Human Rights,* 08.07.2020

[16] Robbins, L., 'EXCLUSIVE: New UN LGBTI watchdog talks global progress, backlash', 05.11.2018, *Washington Blade*

[17] 'Banning conversion therapy', Response submitted to UK Government Consultation, January 2022, Equalities and Human Right Commission

[18] Kennedy, H., Baroness, 'Britain needs clear laws to protect LGBT+ people from conversion therapies', 01.10.2021, *The Guardian*

[19] Kearns, A., MP, 'We must Criminalise the Abhorrent Practice of LGBTQ+ Conversion Therapy', 08.02.21, *Oakham Nub News*

[20] Ibid.

[21] 'It's a Sin: Miniseries', 29.01.2021, *Rotten Tomatoes*

[22] Kearns, A., MP, 'We must Criminalise the Abhorrent Practice of LGBTQ+ Conversion Therapy', op. cit.

[23] Brinton. S., 'I was Tortured in Gay Conversion Therapy. And It's still Legal in 41 States', 24.01.2018, *The New York Times*

[24] Scott, A.O., Review: 'The Miseducation of Cameron Post: Resists the Straight and Narrow', 02.08.2018, *The New York Times*

[25] 'Boy Erased', Film Reviews, 08.02.2019, *The Times*

[26] Kennedy, H., Baroness, 'Britain needs clear laws ...', op. cit.

[27] https://www.wnd.com/2013/03/transgendered-woman-lies-about-therapy-torture/#soT53CzpvAh4AeCw.99

[28] Nicol, P., 'Stephen Fry's Edwardian Secrets review – an exposé of Edward VII', 15.08.2021, *The Sunday Times*

[29] 'Government brings LGBT charity leaders together to grow the sector', 05.02.2020; and Government Equalities Office and Baroness Williams of Trafford, Minister for Equalities, Baroness Williams speaking at the Government Equalities Office's LGBT Leadership Summit, 05.02.2020, GOV.UK

[30] LGBT Action Plan, Improving the lives of Lesbian, Gay, Bisexual and Transgender People, Government Equalities Office and the Rt Hon Penny Mordaunt MP, 03.07.2018

[31] House of Commons criticised after asking if 'gay cure' therapy should be illegal, 03.07.2020, House of Commons@ HouseofCommons

32 Laura Russell, statement to LBC News, 03.07.2020

33 https://t.co/BDgxOaU7S8 MunroeBergdorf, 03.08.2020

34 Kirkup, J., 'The document that reveals the remarkable tactics of trans lobbyists', 03.12.2019, *Coffee House, The Spectator* commenting on: 'Only adults? Good practices in legal gender recognition for youth, a report on the current state of laws and NGO advocacy in eight countries in Europe, with a focus on rights of young people', IGLYO, Thomson Reuters Foundation, Dentons, November 2019

35 Murray, D., 'Preaching to the Converted, The fake fight against 'gay' therapy', 27.03.2021, *The Spectator*

36 Murphy, S., 'Three LGBT advisors quit over 'hostile environment' concerns', 11.03.2021, *The Times*

37 Parker, J., Government's LGBT advisory panel disbanded, *BBC News*, 14.04.202

38 Murphy, S., 'Three LGBT advisers quit …', op. cit., https://youtu. be/vl38dzzn1wc (08.03.2020). Transcript: https://hansard. parliament.uk/commons/2021-03-08

39 Ozanne, J., 'As a lesbian woman, I was subjected to conversion practices…', 01.04.2022, *The Guardian*

40 Roberts, M., 'In praise of conversion', 28.10.2021, *Artillery Row, The Critic*

41 Turner, J., 'Banning gay conversion therapy is a minefield', 15.05.2021, *The Times*

42 Olson-Kennedy, J., 'When the Human Toll of Conversion Therapy Is Not Enough', *JAMA Pediatrics,* published online, 07.03.2022

43 Forsythe, A. et al., 'Humanistic and Economic Burden of Conversion Therapy Among LGBTQ Youths in the United States', *JAMA Pediatrics,* published online 07.03.2022.

44 Olson-Kennedy. J., 'When the Human Toll of Conversion Therapy …', op. cit.

45 'Banning Conversion Therapy', Response submitted …, op. cit.

46 Jones, S.L., 'Sexual Orientation and Reason: On the Implications of False Beliefs about Homosexuality', January 2012, Wheaton College (Illinois)

47 Davidson, M.R, Moseley, C. and Rosik, C.H., A Response to the UK Government's Intended Ban on Therapeutic Choice. 2018. IFTCC.org

[48] Walker, M.D., When Clients Want Your Help to "Pray Away the Gay": Implications for Couple and Family Therapists. J of Feminist Family Therapy 2013: 25(2) 112-134

[49] Cunningham, T., 'Scarred by the gay conversion zealots: Electrocuted, exorcised, and beaten. As a new law is unveiled to outlaw barbaric 'therapy' to make gay people straight, four victims bravely tell of their experiences', *The Daily Mail*, 11.05.2021

[50] Collins J. and Palmer, A. 'Google drops LGBT+ Conversion Therapy', *Daily Mail.com*, 29.03.2019

[51] De Lacy, M., 'Cure me, I'm gay! Embarrassing Bodies', Dr Christian Jessen will test controversial 'reparative' therapy in C4 documentary, 23.01.2014, *The Daily Mail*

[52] Murray, D., 'Preaching to the Converted. The fake fight against 'gay' therapy', 27.03.2021, *The Spectator*

[53] 'Banning Conversion Therapy', Presented to Parliament by the Secretary of State …, op. cit.

[54] Cunningham, T., 'Scarred by the gay conversion zealots …', op. cit.

[55] Scottish Parliament's Equalities, Human Rights and Civil Justice Committee, op. cit.

[56] The Cooper Report, 'Recommendations on legislating effectively for a ban on conversion practices by the ban on 'conversion therapy' legal forum', commissioned by the Ozanne Foundation, October 2021

[57] Chalke, S., Sansbury, I. and Streeter G., 'In the Name of Love: The Church, exclusion and LGB mental health issue', *Oasis Foundation*, 2017, 'Gay activist claims she was spiritually abused by evangelical churches', 23.06.17, *The Guardian*; also, Ozanne, J., 'Spiritual abuse – the next great scandal for the Church', *Royal College of Psychiatrists*, 2017

[58] Galop's CEO Leni Morris, speaking to Cunningham, T., 'Scarred by the gay conversion zealots: Electrocuted, exorcised, and beaten. As a new law is unveiled to outlaw barbaric 'therapy' to make gay people straight, four victims bravely tell of their experiences', 11.05.2021, *The Daily Mail*

[59] Kearns, A., MP: 'We Must Criminalise the Abhorrent Practice of LGBTQ+ Conversion Therapy', op. cit.

[60] 'The Health of Lesbian, Gay, Bisexual, and Transgender People: Building a Foundation for Better Understanding', Institute

of Medicine (US) Committee on Lesbian, Gay, Bisexual, and Transgender Health Issues and Research Gaps and Opportunities, Washington (DC), National Academies Press (US), 2011

61 National LGBT Survey, Summary Report 2018, Government Equalities Office

62 Jowett, A., et al., 'Conversion therapy: an evidence assessment and qualitative study', 29.10.21, Government Equalities Office and Equality Hub

63 Smith, G., Bartlett, A. and King, M., 'Treatments of homosexuality in Britain since the 1950s – an oral history: the experience of patients', BMJ, 2004, 02.21: 328 (7437), 427

64 Hunte, B., Gay 'conversion therapy': Man given electric shocks demands apology; O'Neill, B., Criminalising Parental Love, *Spiked,* 22.01.2022; LGBT correspondent, *BBC News,* 16.12.2020

65 Murphy, S., 'Three LGBT advisers quit over 'hostile environment' concerns', 11.03.2021, *The Times*

66 Murray, D., 'Preaching to the converted', op. cit.

67 Cunningham, T., 'Scarred by the gay conversion zealots …', op. cit.

68 Adam Jowett, A. et al., 'Conversion therapy: an evidence assessment and qualitative study', op. cit.

69 Ozanne, J., 'The UK must ban 'conversion therapy' – even for adults who claim to want it', 02.11.2021, *The Guardian*

70 Wells, K. and Schiavo, N. Scottish Parliament's Equalities, Human Rights and Civil Justice Committee 'Conversion Therapy in Canada: The Roles and Responsibilities of Municipalities', MacEwan University, Canada, October 2019

71 Yarhouse, M.A., 'When Clients Seek Treatment for Same-Sex Attraction: Ethical Issues in the "Right to Choose" Debate', *Psychotherapy,* 1998, 35, 248-259

72 Memorandum of Understanding on Conversion Therapy. Collaborative publication. Version 2. March 2022. Also:The College of Psychiatrists London, 'Statement on sexual orientation', Approved by the Policy Committee, Position Statement PS02/2014, April 2014

73 'Banning Conversion Therapy', presented to Parliament by the Secretary of State …, op. cit.

74 LGBTQ+ Action Plan | Gov.Wales https://gov.wales › lgbtq-action-plan

[75] Yarhouse, M., The battle regarding sexuality. In Cummings, N.C. O'Donahue, W and Cummings, J., eds, *Psychology's War on Religion, 2009*, Phoenix (AZ), Zeig, Tucker & Theisen, Inc.

[76] Glassgold, J.M., American Psychological Association, 2009, Report of the American Psychological Association Task Force on Appropriate Therapeutic Responses to Sexual Orientation, apa.org/pi/lgbc/publications/therapeutic-resp.html

[77] Serovich, J.M. et al., A Systematic Review of the Research Base on Sexual Orientation Therapies, Journal of Marital and Family Therapy. 2008, 34(2), 227-238

[78] Jones, S.L., 'Sexual Orientation and Reason: On the Implications of False Beliefs about Homosexuality, op. cit.

[79] Ibid.

[80] Caspian, J., My Battle with the transgender thought police, Spiked, 22.02.2019

[81] Manning, S., Cancelled by Childline: Ex-barrister lost his role as a volunteer counsellor with the charity after raising fears over the way children confused about their gender are rushed into changing sex, *The Mail on Sunday*, 04.08.2021

[82] Memorandum of Understanding on Conversion Therapy in the UK, bacp.co.uk. Version 1 2017, Version 2 2021; also Royal College of Psychiatrists London, 'Statement on sexual orientation'. Approved by the Policy Committee. Position Statement PS02/2014 April 2014

[83] Shrier, A., 'Gender Activists Are Trying to Cancel My Book. Why is Silicon Valley Helping Them?' 07.11.2020, *Quillette*

[84] 'Memorandum of Understanding on Conversion Therapy', op. cit.

[85] Standards of Care for the Health of Transsexual, Transgender and Gender *Nonconforming People* 2012 [7th Version] World Professional Association for Transgender Health

[86] Bannerman, L., 'Give irreversible gender drugs at age 14, says transgender health group', 17.06.2022, *The Times*

[87] Rajkumar, R.P., 'Gender Identity Disorder and Schizophrenia: Neurodevelopmental Disorders with Common Causal Mechanisms?', *Schizophrenia Research and Treatment*, 2014, Article ID 463757

[88] Nelson, F., 'Transgender children: When doing nothing causes harm', 03.10.2018, *Medical Republic*

[89] Coversheet: 'Prohibiting Conversion Practices ...', Policy Manager, Civil Law and Human Rights Policy Group Ministry

of Justice, 15.04.2021. 'Obviously We Want to Criminalise Parents', Bill advocate, 07.08.2021, *Scoop Regional*

90 Bill C-6, An Act to amend the Criminal Code (conversion therapy)

91 O'Neill, B., 'Criminalising parental love', *Spiked,* 22.01.2022

92 Keenan, J., 'Doctors Insist Canadian 14-Year-Old Needs No Parent Consent for Trans Hormone Injections', *The Federalist,* 26.02.2019

93 Murray, D., 'Preaching to the converted', op. cit.

94 Report on petition PE1817, 'End conversion therapy', op. cit.

95 Forrest, A., 'Boris Johnson abandons plan to ban LGBT conversion therapy', 31.03.2022, *The Independent*. Martin, D., 'Boris goes full-circle on gay conversion ban: Chaos as PM u-turns on u-turn and will now proceed with move to outlaw controversial therapy after backlash when plans were 'quietly dropped'', 31.03.2022, *The Daily Mail;* Wright, O., 'Boris Johnson does double U-turn on LGBT conversion therapy ban', 01.04.2022, *The Times*

96 Ozanne, J., 'As a lesbian woman, I was subjected to conversion practices…', 01.04.2022, *The Guardian*

97 Parris, M., War refugees are being let down at the top, 02.03.2022, The Times

98 Marshall, A., 'Milo comes out as straight, chaste and catholic', *The Spectator,* 10.03.2021

99 Murray, D., *The Madness of Crowds,* Bloomsbury Continuum (2019), 40

100 Tatchell, P., Beyond Equality, The New Humanist, 2001, 116 (1)

101 McCartney, J., 'The new sexual revolution', 17.10.2015, *The Spectator*

102 RSE KS2: 'Identity – Understanding sexual and gender identities' (bbc.co.uk)

103 National Survey on LGBTQ Youth Mental Health, 2019, New York: The Trevor Project

104 Murray, D., *The Madness of Crowds*, op. cit., 43

105 Mayer, L.S, McHugh, P. R., Part One: 'Sexual Orientation, Sexuality and Gender', The New Atlantis, Fall 2016

106 Murray, D., *The Madness of Crowds,* op. cit., 22-23

107 Murray, D., 'Preaching to the Converted. The fake fight against 'gay' therapy', 27.03.2021, *The Spectator*

[108] McCloskey, D., 'I'm a transwoman who signed the Harper's letter with JK Rowling. Here's why', October 2020, *Prospect*

[109] Sharp, R., 'Right-wing provocateur Milo Yiannopoulos declares himself an 'ex-gay' who is 'sodomy free' and wants to un-cancel 'conversion therapy' – but what does his husband think?', *The Daily Mail*, 10.03.2021; Mainwaring, D., 'Activist Milo Yiannopoulos is now 'Ex-Gay', consecrating his life to St. Joseph', 09.03.2021, *LifeSiteNews*

[110] Marshall, A., 'Milo comes out …', op. cit.

[111] National LGBT Survey, Research Report 2018, Government Equalities Office and Rt Hon Penny Mordaunt, MP; also, Summary Report, 2018

[112] Turban, J. L., et al. Psychological attempts to change a person's gender identity from transgender to cisgender: Estimated prevalence across US States, 2015, American Journal of Public Health, 2019. 109(10), 1452-1454

[113] 'Banning Conversion Therapy', presented to Parliament by the Secretary of State ...', op. cit.

[114] Bartlett, A., Smith, G., and King, M., 'The response of mental health professionals to clients seeking help to change or redirect same-sex sexual orientation', *BMC Psychiatry*, 2009, 9(1), 11

[115] Jones, S.L. and Yarhouse, M.A., 'Ex-Gays? An Extended Longitudinal Study of Attempted Religiously Mediated Change in Sexual Orientation', 2011, *ResearchGate*

[116] Rosik, C.H., NARTH response to the WMA statement on natural variations of human sexuality, *Linacre Quarterly*, 2014, 81(2), 111–114; Pela, C. and Sutton, P., 'Sexual attraction fluidity and well-being in men: a therapeutic outcome study', *Journal of Human Sexuality*, 2021, 12, 61-86.

[117] Lambert, M.J., 'The efficacy and effectiveness of psychotherapy …', op. cit.

[118] Blake, N., 'NYC Bans People from Talking to a Therapist about Discomfort with Sex', 01.02.2019, *The Federalist*

[119] Jowett, A. et al., 'Conversion therapy: an evidence assessment and qualitative study', op. cit.

[120] Blake, N., 'NYC Bans People …', op. cit.

[121] Rosik, C.H., 'Sexual orientation change efforts and the campaign to ban them', 16.07.2015, *MercatorNet*

[122] 'Banning Conversion Therapy', presented to Parliament by the Secretary of State…, op. cit.

[123] Wright T., Candy B. and King M., Conversion therapies in transgender people: a systematic review, 2018. 8 (12) *BMJ Open*

[124] (The international coalition group for ex-gay organisations changed its name from 'Positive Alternatives to Homosexuality' (PATH) to 'Positive Approaches to Healthy Sexuality'.)

[125] Dominic Davies, Pink Therapy Blog, 'Curing the gays', posted on April 3, 2014 by Pink Therapy; and from the Department of Health 'Round Table' on Conversion Therapy Training & Policy

[126] Hancock, K.A., Gock, T.S. and Haldeman, D.C., 'Science meets practice in determining effectiveness of sexual orientation change efforts', *American Psychologist,* 2012, 67(6), 499-500

[127] Collins, J. and Palmer. A, 'Google drops LGBT+ Conversion Therapy', *Daily Mail.com* 29.03.2019

[128] https://www.facebook.com/itvnews/videos/piers-morgan-in-angry-row-with-gay-conversion-doctor/10155155724752672/)

[129] Murray, D., *The Madness of Crowds*, op. cit., 17-18

[130] Rosik, C.H., 'Sexual orientation change efforts…', op. cit.

[131] Sullins, D.P., Rosik, C.H., and Santero, P., 'Efficacy and risk of sexual orientation change efforts: a retrospective analysis of 125 exposed men', *F1000Res.* 2021 10:222.

[132] Ibid.

[133] Murray, D., *The Madness of Crowds,* op. cit., 22

[134] Sargent, E., 'Gay conversion therapy: my undercover investigation', 31.07. 2021, *The Times*

[135] Jones, S.L., 'Same-Sex Science', February 2012, https://www.firstthings.com/article/2012/02/same-sex-science

[136] Ganna, A. et al., 'Large-scale GWAS reveals insights into the genetic architecture of same-sex sexual behavior', *Science* 2019: Vol. 365 (6456), 1-8; Mills, M.C., 'How do genes affect same-sex behavior?', *Science* 2019: Vol. 365 (6456), 869-870

[137] Belluck, P., 'Many Genes Influence Same-Sex Sexuality, Not a Single 'Gay Gene', 28.09.19, *The New York Times*

[138] Walker, M.D., 'When Clients Want Your Help to "Pray Away the Gay": Implications for Couple and Family Therapists', *Journal of Feminist Family Therapy,* 2013, 25:2, 112-134

[139] Bartlett, A., Smith, G., and King, M., 'The response of mental health professionals to clients … op. cit.

[140] Kelleher, P., quoting Ozanne. J., 'Boris Johnson says conversion therapy ban won't cover 'prayer for sexual orientation or gender identity', 13.04.2021, *Pink News.*

[141] Cowburn, A., 'Boris Johnson accused of creating a loophole' in proposed conversion therapy ban', 15.04.2021, *The Independent*

[142] Kelley, N., interview by Kelleher, P. Boris Johnson says conversion therapy ban won't cover 'prayer for sexual orientation or gender identity',13.04.2021, *Pink News*

[143] Lord Herbert, speaking to Tom Newton Dunn, 'Britain needs more trans people in public life, including the Commons', 03.07.2021, *The Times*

[144] Jowett, A. et al., 'Conversion therapy: an evidence assessment and qualitative study', op. cit.

[145] Roberts, M., 'In praise of conversion', op. cit.

[146] 'The ex-gay files: the bizarre world of gay-to-straight conversion', 01.02.2010, *The Independent*

[147] Strudwick, P., 'Conversion therapy: she tried to make me 'pray the gay away'', 27.05.2011, *The Guardian*

[148] Geen, J., 'Campaign launched to expose ex-gay therapists', 10.02.2010, *Pink News;* also, Strudwick P., 'Psychotherapist who tried to 'cure' me of homosexuality has at last been struck off', 04.10.2012, *The Independent*

[149] Ozanne, J., 'Spiritual abuse – the next great scandal for the Church', Royal College of Psychiatrists, 2017, https://www. rcpsych.ac.uk/docs/default-source/members/sigs/spirituality-spsig/spsig-archive-ozanne-spiritual-abuse-the-next-great-scandal-for-the-church.pdf?sfvrsn. See also: Sherwood. H., 'C of E bishop backs prosecution of those who defy gay conversion ban', 09.06.2021, *The Guardian*

[150] Government Equalities Office Consultation, 'Banning conversion therapy': Response from LGBT Humanists UK', 23.11.2021

[151] Rouncivell, G., 'Church leaders in Lancaster and Morecambe among those to sign government letter opposing 'conversion therapy' ban', 01.03.2022, *Lancaster Guardian*

[152] Griffin, L. et al., 'Sex, gender and gender identity: a re-evaluation of the evidence. *BJPsych Bulletin*. Published online by Cambridge University Press: 21.07.2020

[153] Jowett, A. et al., 'Conversion therapy: an evidence assessment and qualitative study, op. cit.

154 Wells, K. and Schiavo, N., Conversion Therapy in Canada…, op. cit.

155 Scottish Parliament's Equalities, Human Rights and Civil Justice Committee, PE1817: End Conversion Therapy Scottish Parliament's Equalities, Human Rights and Civil Justice Committee, 16.07.2020

156 Glassgold, J.M., American Psychological Association, 2009, Report of the American Psychological Association Task Force, op. cit.

157 Jones, S.L. and Yarhouse, M.A., 'Ex-Gays?, An Extended Longitudinal Study…', op. cit.

158 Lambert, M. J. The efficacy and effectiveness of psychotherapy, in M. J. Lambert (Ed.), *Bergin and Garfield's Handbook of Psychotherapy and Behavior Change* (6th ed.) 2013. Hoboken, NJ, Wiley

159 Rosik, C.H., 'Sexual orientation change efforts …', op. cit.

160 Jowett, A. et al., 'Conversion therapy: an evidence assessment and qualitative study', op. cit.

161 Sullins, D.P., Rosik, C.H., and Santero, P., 'Efficacy and risk of sexual orientation change efforts', op. cit.

162 Ortiz, R., Gilgoff, R. and Burke Harris, N., 'Adverse Childhood Experiences, Toxic Stress, and Trauma-Informed Neurology', *JAMA Neurology* 2022; 79(6): 539-540.

163 Sullins, D.P., Rosik, C.H. and Santero, P., 'Efficacy and risk of sexual orientation change efforts', op. cit.

164 Jones, S.L., 'Sexual Orientation and Reason …', op. cit.

165 D'Augelli, A.R., Grossman A.H., Hershberger S.L. and O'Connell, T.S., 'Aspects of mental health among older lesbian, gay and bisexual adults', *Aging & Mental Health*, 2001, 5(2), 149-158

166 D'Augelli, A.R. et al., 'Aspects of mental health among older lesbian, gay and bisexual adults', op. cit.

167 2018 National Faith and Sexuality Survey, 20.02.2019, Ozanne Foundation

168 Ould, P., Church Teaching and LGB mental health,' *Psephizo*, 13.02.2017 https://www.psephizo.com/sexuality-2/church-teaching-and-lgb-mental-health/

169 Link, B.G, et al., 'Measuring mental illness stigma', *Schizophrenia Bulletin* 2004; 30: 511-541; also, Corrigan, P.W. and Watson,

A.C., 'The paradox of self-stigma and mental illness', *Journal of Clinical Psychology*, 2002, 9, 35-53

[170] Stevelink, S., 'The psychometric assessment of internalised stigma instruments: a systematic review', *Stigma, Research & Action*, 2012, 2(2), 100-118

[171] Frost, D.M and Meyer, I.H., 'Internalized homophobia and relationship quality...', quoting Hughes M. and Thomas M.E., 'The continuing significance of race revisited: A study of race, class, and quality of life in America', *American Sociological Review*, 1998, 63, 785-795

[172] Kertzner, R.M. et al., 'Social and Psychological Well-being in Lesbians, Gay Men, and Bisexuals: The Effects of Race, Gender, Age, and Sexual Identity', *American Journal of Orthopsychiatry*, 2009, 79(4), 500-510

[173] Serovich, J.M. A Systematic Review of the Research Base on Sexual Reorientation Therapies. *Journal of Marital and Family Therapy*, 2008, 34(2), 227-38

[174] Spitzer, R. L., 'Can some gay men and lesbians change their sexual orientation? 200 participants reporting a change from homosexual to heterosexual orientation.' *Archives of Sexual Behavior*, 2003, 32(5), 403-17

[175] Spitzer, R. L., Spitzer reassesses his 2003 study of reparative therapy of homosexuality *Archives of Sexual Behavior*, 2012, 41(4), 757-757

[176] Armelli, J.A., et al., A response to Spitzer's (2012) reassessment of his 2003 study of reparative therapy of homosexuality. *Archives of Sexual Behavior*, 2013, 41, 1335-1336

[177] Jones, S.L and Yarhouse, M.A., 'Ex-Gays?: An Extended Longitudinal Study...', op. cit.

[178] Ibid.

[179] Jones, S.L and Yarhouse, M.A., 'A Longitudinal Study of Attempted Religiously Mediated Sexual Orientation Change', *Journal of Sex and Marital Therapy*, 2011, 37, 404-427

[180] Jowett, A. et al., 'Conversion therapy: an evidence assessment and qualitative study...' op. cit.

[181] Krueger, E.A. et al., '*Generations – A Study of the Life and Health of LGB People in a Changing Society (Methodology and Technical Notes, Gallup Quantitative Survey)*', 2020, The Williams Institute, Los Angeles, CA

[182] Blosnich, J.R. et al., 'Sexual orientation change efforts, adverse childhood experiences and suicide ideation and attempt among sexual minority adults, United States, 2016-2018', *American Journal of Public Health*, 2020, 110(7), 1024-1030

[183] Blosnich, J.R. et al. respond, *American Journal of Public Health* 2021, 111, e20–e21

[184] Rosik, C.H., 'Sexual orientation change efforts ...' op. cit.

[185] For example: Ryan, C. et al., 'Parent-initiated sexual orientation change efforts with LGBT adolescents: Implications for young adult mental health and adjustment', *Journal of Homosexuality*, 2018, 67(2), 159-17

[186] Salway, T. et al. 'Prevalence of exposure to sexual orientation change efforts and associated sociodemographic characteristics and psychosocial health outcomes among Canadian sexual minority men', *The Canadian Journal of Psychiatry*, 2020, 65(7), 502-509

[187] Turban, J. L. et al, 'Psychological attempts to change a person's gender identity from transgender to cisgender: Estimated prevalence across US States, 2015', *American Journal of Public Health*, 2019, 109(10), 1452-1454

[188] Turban, J. et al., Association Between Recalled Exposure to Gender Identity Conversion Efforts and Psychological Distress and Suicide Attempts Among Transgender Adults, *JAMA Psychiatry* 2020, 77(1), 68-76

[189] Schneeberger, A.R. et al., 'Stressful childhood experiences and health outcomes in sexual minority populations: a systematic review', *Social Psychiatry and Psychiatry Epidemiology*, 2014, 49(9), 1427-45

[190] Wilson, H.W. and Widom, C.S. 'Does physical abuse, sexual abuse, or neglect in childhood increase the likelihood of same-sex sexual relationships and cohabitation? A prospective 30-year follow-up', *Archives of Sexual Behavior*, 2010, 39(1), 63-74

[191] Rosik, C.H. et al., Sexual Orientation Change Efforts, Adverse Childhood Experiences, and Suicidality, *American Journal of Public Health*, 2021, 111(4), e19-e20; Sullins, D., 'Sexual orientation change efforts (soce) *reduce* suicide: correcting a false research narrative', 16.03.2021, https://ssrn.com/abstract=3729353 or http://dx.doi.org/10.2139/ssrn.3729353

[192] Rajkumar, R.P., 'Gender Identity Disorder and Schizophrenia...', op. cit.

[193] Sullins, D. P., 'Absence of Behavioral Harm Following Non-efficacious Sexual Orientation Change Efforts: A Retrospective Study of United States Sexual Minority Adults, 2016-2018', *Frontiers in Psychology*, 02.02.2022

[194] Pachankis, J.E. et al., LGB-Affirmative Cognitive-Behavioral Therapy for Young Adult Gay and Bisexual Men: A Randomized Controlled Trial of a Transdiagnostic Minority Stress Approach, *Journal of Consulting and Clinical Psychology*, 2015, 83(5), 875-889

[195] Barlow, D.H. et al., *Unified protocol for transdiagnostic treatment of emotional disorders: Therapist guide,* Oxford University Press, 2010

[196] Pachankis, J.E. et al., A transdiagnostic minority stress intervention for gender diverse sexual minority women's depression, anxiety, and unhealthy alcohol use: A randomized controlled trial. *Journal of Consulting and Clinical Psychology, 2020, 88*(7), 613-630

[197] Pachankis, J.E. et al., LGB-Affirmative Cognitive-Behavioral Therapy…, op. cit.

[198] Pachankis, J.E. et al., 'Sexual orientation concealment and mental health: A conceptual and meta-analytic review', *Psychology Bulletin,* 2020, 146(10), 831-871

[199] Pachankis, J.E. et al., 'LGB-Affirmative Cognitive-Behavioral Therapy for Young Adult Gay and Bisexual Men: A Randomized Controlled Trial of a Transdiagnostic Minority Stress Approach', *Journal of Consulting and Clinical Psychology,* 2015, 83(5), 875-889

[200] Jones, S.L and Yarhouse, M.A., 'A Longitudinal Study of Attempted Religiously Mediated Sexual Orientation Change', op. cit., 404-427

[201] Regnerus, M. and Vermurlen, B., 'Attitudes in the U.S. Toward Hormonal and/or Surgical Interventions for Adolescents Experiencing Gender Dysphoria', *Archives of Sexual Behavior,* 28.01.2022

[202] Sullins, D.P, Rosik, C.H and Santero, P., 'Efficacy and risk of sexual orientation change efforts…', op. cit.

[203] Karten, E.Y. and Wade, J.C., 'Sexual orientation change efforts in men: A client perspective.' *Journal of Men's Studies,* 2010, 18(1), 84-102

[204] Dehlin, J.P. et al., 'Sexual orientation change efforts among current or former LDS church members', *Journal of Counseling Psychology*, 2014, 62(2), 95

[205] Lefevor, G. T. et al., 'Same-sex attracted, not LGBQ: the associations of sexual identity labeling on religiousness, sexuality, and health among Mormons', *Journal of Homosexuality,* 2020, 67, 940-964

[206] Robins, A. and Fiske, A., 'Explaining the Relation between Religiousness and Reduced Suicidal Behavior: Social Support Rather Than Specific Beliefs', *Suicide and Life-Threatening Behavior,* 2009, Vol 39 (4), 386-395

[207] Kralovec, K. et al., 'Religion and suicide risk in lesbian, gay and bisexual Australians', *Journal of Religion and Health*, 2012, 53, 413-423

[208] Shilo, G. and Savaya, R., 'Mental health of lesbian, gay, and bisexual youth and young adults: Differential effects of age, gender, religiosity, and sexual orientation, *Journal of Research on Adolescence,* 2012, 22, 310-325; Barnes, D.M. and Meyer, I., 'Religious affiliation, internalized homophobia, and mental health in lesbians, gay men, and bisexuals', *American Journal of Orthopsychiatry,* 2012, 82, 505-515; Harris, J.I. et al., 'Religious attitudes, internalized homophobia, and identity in gay and lesbian adults', *Journal of Gay and Lesbian Mental Health,* 2008, 12, 205-225

[209] Shearer, A. et al., 'Religion, Sexual Orientation, and Suicide Attempts Among a Sample of Suicidal Adolescents', *Journal of Suicide and Life-Threatening Behavior*, 2018, 48(4), 431-43

[210] Meyer I.H., Teylan M. and Schwartz S., 'The role of help-seeking in preventing suicide attempts among lesbians, gay men, and bisexuals', *Journal of Suicide and Life-Threatening Behavior*, 2015, 45(1), 25-36

[211] Barnes, D.M. and Meyer, I.H., 'Religious Affiliation, Internalized Homophobia, and Mental Health in Lesbians, Gay Men, and Bisexuals', American Journal of Orthopsychiatry, 2012, 82(4), 505-515

[212] Walker, R. L. et al., 'Perceived racism and suicide ideation: Mediating role of depression but moderating role of religiosity among African American adults', *Journal of Suicide and Life-Threatening Behavior*, 2014, 44, 548-559

[213] Kertzner, R.M., et al., 'Social and psychological well-being in lesbians, gay men, and bisexuals: The effects of race, gender, age, and sexual identity'. *American Journal of Orthopsychiatry,* 2009, 79(4), 500-510; Barnes, D.M. and Meyer, I.H., 'Religious

Affiliation, Internalized Homophobia, and Mental Health in Lesbians, Gay Men, and Bisexuals', *American Journal of Orthopsychiatry*, 2012, 82(4), 505-515

[214] Barnes, D.M. and Meyer, I., 'Religious affiliation …', Ibid.

[215] Rosik, C.H., Lefevor, G.T. and Beckstead, A.L., 'Sexual Minorities who Reject an LGB Identity: Who Are They and Why Does It Matter?' *Issues in Law and Medicine,* 2021, 36(1), 27-43; Beckstead A.L. and Morrow, S., 'Mormon Clients' Experiences of Conversion Therapy: The Need for a New Treatment Approach', *The Counselling Psychologist,* 2004, 32(5), 651-690

[216] Gibbs, J. J. and Goldbach, J., 'Religious Conflict, Sexual Identity, and Suicidal Behaviors among LGBT Young Adults', *Archives of Suicide Research,* 2015, 19:4, 472-488

[217] Kertzner, R.M. et al., 'Social and psychological wellbeing in lesbians, gay men, and bisexuals: The effects of race, gender, age, and sexual identity'. *American Journal of Orthopsychiatry,* 2009, 79(4), 500-510

[218] Gibbs, J.J. and Goldbach. J, 'Religious Conflict, Sexual Identity …', op. cit.

[219] Beckstead, A. L., 'Cures versus Choices: Agendas in Sexual Reorientation Therapy', *Journal of Gay & Lesbian Psychotherapy,* 2002, 5(3-4), 87-115

[220] Yarhouse, M.A. and Burkett, L.A., 'An inclusive response to LGB and conservative religious persons: The case of same-sex attraction and behavior', *Professional Psychology: Research and Practice,* 2002, 33, 235-241

[221] Tozer, E.E. and Haynes, J.A., 'Why Do Individuals Seek Conversion Therapy? The Role of Religiosity, Internalized Homonegativity, and Identity Development', *The Counselling Psychologist,* 2004, 32(5), 716-740

[222] Walker, M.D., 'When Clients Want Your Help to "Pray Away the Gay": Implications for Couple and Family Therapists', *Journal of Feminist Family Therapy,* 2013: 25(2) 112-134, quoting Yarhouse, M. A. and Burkett, L. A. (2002). An inclusive response to LGB and conservative religious persons: The case of same-sex attraction and behavior. *Professional Psychology: Research and Practice, 33*(3), 235-241

[223] Beckstead, A. L., 'Cures versus Choices…', op. cit.

[224] Jones, S.L., 'Sexual orientation and reason: On the implications of false beliefs about homosexuality', op. cit.

[225] Dickson, N. et al., 'Stability and Change in Same-Sex Attraction, Experience and Identity by Sex and Age in a New Zealand Cohort', *Archives of Sexual Behaviour*, 2013, 43(5), 753-63

[226] Harris, K.M. and Udry, J.R., 'National Longitudinal Study of Adolescent to Adult Health (Add Health), 1994-2008', Carolina Population Center, University of North Carolina at Chapel Hill, Inter-university Consortium for Political and Social Research, 2018-08-06. https://doi.org/10.3886/ICPSR21600.v21

[227] Savin-Williams, R.C. and Ream, G.L., 'Prevalence and stability of sexual orientation components during adolescence and young adulthood', *Archives of Sexual Behaviour*, 2007, 36(3), 385-94

[228] Dickson, N., et al., 'Stability and change in same-sex attraction, experience, and identity...', op. cit.

[229] Geary, R.S. et al., 'Sexual identity, attraction and behaviour in Britain: The implications of using different dimensions of sexual orientation to estimate the size of sexual minority populations and inform public health interventions', *PLOS One,* 2018, 13(1)

[230] Laumann, E.O. et al., *The Social Organisation of Sexuality*, University of Chicago Press, 1994

[231] Diamond, L.M. *Sexual Fluidity: Understanding Women's Love and Desire*, Harvard University Press, 2009

[232] General Social Survey, University of Chicago, 2020

[233] Kinnish, K.K., Strassberg D.S., and Turner C.W., 'Sex differences in the flexibility of sexual orientation: a multidimensional retrospective assessment', *Archives of Sexual Behaviour,* 2005, 34(2),173-83

[234] McCabe, J., Brewster, K.L. and Tillman, K.H., 'Patterns and correlates of same-sex sexual activity among U.S. teenagers and young adults' *Perspectives on Sexual and Reproductive Health,* 2011 September, 43(3), 142-50

[235] Kinnish K.K., Strassberg D.S. and Turner C.W., 'Sex differences in the flexibility of sexual orientation: a multidimensional retrospective assessment', *Archives of Sexual Behaviour*, 2005 April, 34(2), 173-83

[236] Michael Bailey, J., 'What is Sexual Orientation and Do Women Have One?', *Nebraska Symposium,* https://www.researchgate.net/publication/24028378

[237] LGBT+ Pride, 2021 Global Survey points to a generation gap around gender identity and sexual attraction. IPSOS, 2021

[238] https://mercatornet.com/the-number-of-lgbt-americans-is-soaring- why/77778/#:~:text=As%20one%20digs,as%20they%20are.%E2%80%9D

[239] Herman, J.L., Flores, A.R., and O'Neill, K.K., 'How Many Adults and Youth Identify As Transgender In The United States?' Williams Institute, UCLA, 2022

[240] Brown, A. 'About 5% of young adults in the U.S. say their gender is different from their sex assigned at birth', Pew Research Center, 2022

[241] 'Sexual orientation, UK: 2020, Experimental Statistics on sexual orientation in the UK in 2020 by region, sex, age, marital or legal partnership status, ethnic group and socio-economic classification, using data from the Annual Population Survey (APS)', ONS, 25.05.2022.

[242] Mercer, Catherine H. et al., 'Changes in sexual attitudes and lifestyles in Britain through the life course and over time: findings from the National Surveys of Sexual Attitudes and Lifestyles (Natsal)', The Lancet, 2013: 382 (9907), 1781–1794

[243] Johnson, A.M. et al., 'Natsal 2000: Sexual behaviour in Britain: partnerships, practices, and HIV risk behaviours', The Lancet, 2001, 358 (9296), 1835-42; Wellings, K. et al., 'Sexual behaviour in Britain: early heterosexual experience', The Lancet, 2001, 358 (9296), 1843-50; Godeau, E. et al., 'Contraceptive Use by 15-Year-Old Students at Their Last Sexual Intercourse: Results from 24 Countries'. Archives of Pediatrics and Adolescent Medicine, 2008, 162(1), 66-73

[244] ONS Statistical Bulletin: Sexual identity, UK, 2016, 'Experimental Official Statistics on sexual identity in the UK in 2016 by region, sex, age, marital status, ethnicity and National Statistics Socio-economic Classification'.

[245] For example, Diamond, L.M. and Rosky, C.J., 'Scrutinizing Immutability: Research on Sexual Orientation and U.S. Legal Advocacy for Sexual Minorities', J. Sex Res. 2016, 53(4-5), 363-91; Savin-Williams, R. C., Joyner, K., and Rieger G., 'Prevalence and stability of self-reported sexual orientation identity during young adulthood', Archives of Sexual Behavior, 2012, 41, 103-110

[246] Parkes, A. et al., 'Comparison of Teenagers' Early Same-Sex and Heterosexual Behavior: UK Data from the SHARE and RIPPLE Studies', Journal of Adolescent Health, 02.09.2010

[247] Floyd, F.J. and Bakeman, R., 'Coming-out across the life course: implications of age and historical context', *Archives of Sexual Behaviour*, 2006, 35(3), 287-96

[248] Burton, C.M. et al., Sexual Minority-Related Victimization as a Mediator of Mental Health Disparities in Sexual Minority Youth: A Longitudinal Analysis', *Journal of Youth and Adolescence,* 2013, 42(3), 394-402

[249] Parris, M., 'It's clear our sexuality isn't set in stone', 27.02.2021, *The Times*

[250] Silva, T.A., 'Quantitative Test of Critical Heterosexuality Theory: Predicting Straight Identification in a Nationally Representative Sample', *Sexuality Research and Social Policy,* 2018, 15, 353-366

[251] Rosario, M. et al., 'Sexual identity development among gay, lesbian, and bisexual youths: consistency and change over time' *Journal of Sex Research,* 2006, 43(1), 46-58

[252] Sullins, D.P., Rosik, C.H and Santero, P., 'Efficacy and risk of sexual orientation change efforts…', op. cit.

[253] Rosik, C.H. et al., 'Sexual Orientation Change Efforts…', op. cit.

[254] Saunders, R., 'Did Boris kill Conservatism? 07.06.2022, *Unherd*

[255] Jones, S.L., Sexual Orientation and Reason, op. cit.

[256] Murray, D., 'How Stonewall was Exposed', 22.10.2021, *Unherd*

[257] Memorandom of Understanding on Conversion Therapy in the UK. Version 2 – Update March 2022

[258] Consensus Statement. At the request of the Department of Health, this public information was prepared by the UK Council for Psychotherapy with the support and assistance of the British Psychoanalytic Council, the Royal College of Psychiatrists, the British Association for Counselling and Psychotherapy, the British Psychological Society, The National Counselling Society, Pink Therapy, Stonewall, PACE and Relate, June 2014

[259] Quoted by Crist, C., 'Transgender people in the U.S still face conversion therapy attempts', 05.09.2019, Reuters. Source: https://bit.ly/2kjmRej American Journal of Public Health, 15.08.2019

[260] Ozanne, J., Conversion Therapy, *Letters,* 21.05.2021, *The Times,* referring to Turner, J. 'Banning gay conversion therapy …', op. cit.

[261] Dr Poulter, 14.01.2014, Column 706, *Hansard*, House of Commons

262 Provost Kelvin Holdsworth played a key role in campaigning for the legalisation of same-sex marriage in Scottish Episcopal churches; he stood as a Lib Dem candidate in 2005 and wanted school children to be allowed to drop out of "nationalist, sectarian, sexist and homophobic" football and athletics; Burgess, K., 'Anglican minister Kelvin Holdsworth: pray Prince George is gay', 01.12.2017, *The Times*

263 Murray, D., *The Madness of Crowds,* op. cit., p.24

264 Ibid.

265 Roberts, G., Councillor, *Showing Pride,* 11.07.2019, Richmond. gov.uk

266 Somerville, L.H., Jones R.M. and Casey, B.J., 'A time of change: behavioral and neural correlates of adolescent sensitivity to appetitive and aversive environmental cues', *Brain and Cognition*, 2010, 72(1), 124-33

267 Splete, H., 'Few Children Who Socially Transition Soon Change Their Minds'. *Medscape.* 04.05.2022, referring to Olson, K.R. et al., 'Gender Identity 5 Years After Social Transition', *Paediatrics*, 2022; doi: 10.1542/peds.2021-056082

268 O'Neill, B. 'Same-sex marriage: coercion dolled up as civil rights', 30.04.2014, *Spiked Online*

269 Ibid.

270 Krupat, K., 'Out at Work: Building a Gay-Labor Alliance'. University of Minnesota Press, 2001; Berlant, E. and Warner, M., 'Sex in Public', *Critical Inquiry,* 1998, 24(2) 547-566

271 25.04.1999, *The Observer*

272 Lorber, J., quoted in Greer, G., *The Whole Woman,* London, Doubleday 1999, 324

273 'Creating an LGBT inclusive curriculum, a guide for secondary schools' 2017, Stonewall, Relationships Education, Relationships and Sex Education (RSE) and Health Education. 2019, Department of Education.

274 (https://gids.nhs.uk/number-referrals), Gilligan, A. 'Tavistock clinic reveals surge in girls switching gender', 30.06.2019, *The Times;* 'The Surge in Referral Rates of Girls to the Tavistock Continues to Rise', 2019, *Transgender Trend* https://www. transgendertrend.com/surge-referral-rates-girls-tavistock-continues-rise/

275 Ward, V., 'BBC told to put more gays on children's TV', 14.12.2012, *Daily Television*

[276] Pessin-Whedbee, B. *Who are You? The Kid's Guide to Gender Identity*, Jessica Kingsley Publishers, 2017

[277] 'Supporting Transgender Pupils In Schools: Guidance for Scottish Schools', Cabinet Secretary for Education and Skills, August 2021, Scottish Government; also, Blackley, M., 'Scotland will let pupils change gender aged four without their parents' consent – and tells teachers not to question a child's request to choose a new name or use a different toilet', 12.08.2021, *The Daily Mail*

[278] Flynn, S., Wyoming senator booed during graduate speech at alma mater after 'two sexes' comment. 16.05.2022, *The Independent*

[279] Lord Herbert, speaking to Tom Newton Dunn. 'Britain needs more trans people in public life, including the Commons', 03.07.2021, *The Times*

[280] Tatchell, *Letters,* 10.04.2022, *The Times*

[281] Turner, J., 'Each boy's bedroom is a museum of childhood', 06.04.2022, *The Times*

[282] Wallen, M.S.C. and Cohen-Kettens, P.T., 'Psychological outcome of gender dysphoric children', *Journal of the American Academy of Child and Adolescent Psychiatry*, 2008, 47(19), 363-369

[283] Lee, G., 'How many children are going to gender identity clinics in the UK?' FactCheck Q & A, 24.10. 2017.

[284] Nelson, F., 'Transgender children: When doing nothing causes harm', 03.10.2018, *Medical Republic*

[285] Hoyle, A., 'Should Dexter, 9, really be on the transgender fast track? Child who was born a girl has been waiting three years for an autism diagnosis. Yet it took just months for UK's leading gender clinic to agree to set him on road to transitioning', 14.07.2020, *The Daily Mail*

[286] Klink, D. et al., 'Bone mass in young adulthood following gonadotropin-releasing hormone analog treatment and cross-sex hormone treatment in adolescents with gender dysphoria', *Journal of Clinical Endocrinology and Metabolism*, 2015, 100(2)

[287] Duck-Chong, L., 'Rapid-onset gender dysphoria' is a poisonous lie used to discredit trans people', 21.10.2018, *The Guardian*

[288] https://www.ihmistenkirjo.net/blog/psychiatrist-gender-dysphoria-spreads-like-an-epidemic-online

[289] Littman L., 'Rapid-onset gender dysphoria in adolescents and young adults: A study of parental reports', *PLOS One,*

August 2018. Available at https://journals.plos.org/plosone/article?id=10.1371/journal.pone.0202330

[290] 'Psychiatrist: gender dysphoria spreads like an epidemic online', Sven Román, *Kirjo* blog 21.09.2029, first published in *Dagens Nyheter, 13.09.2019*

[291] Van der Miesen, A.I.R. et al., 'Autistic symptoms in children and adolescents with gender dysphoria', *Journal of Autism and Developmental Disorders,* 2018, 48, 1537-48

[292] Stagg, S.D. and Vincent, J., 'Autistic traits in individuals self-defining as transgender or nonbinary', *European Psychiatry: The Journal of the Association of European Psychiatrists*, 2019, 61,17-22; Nobili et al., 'Autistic Traits in Treatment-Seeking Transgender Adults, *Journal of Autism and Developmental Disorders*, 2018, 48(12), 3984-3994; Jones R.M. et al, 'Brief report: female-to-male transsexual people and autistic traits', *Journal of Autism and Developmental Disorders,* 2012, 42, 301-306

[293] De Vries, A.L. et al, 'Autism spectrum disorders in gender dysphoric children and adolescents', *Journal of Autism and Developmental Disorders,* 2010, 40, 930-936

[294] Heylens, G. et al, 'Psychiatric characteristics in transsexual individuals: multicentre study in four European countries', 2014, 204(2), 151-156; Mueller, S.C. et al, 'Transgender Research in the 21st Century: A Selective Critical Review from a Neurocognitive Perspective', *American Journal of Psychiatry,* 2017, 174 (12), 1155-1162

[295] Kaltiala-Heino, R., 'Two years of gender identity service for minors: overrepresentation of natal girls with severe problems in adolescent development', *Child and Adolescent Psychiatry and Mental Health,* 2015, 9(9)

[296] Clarke, A. and Spiliadis, A., 'Taking the Lid Off the Box: The Value of Extended Clinical Assessment for Adolescents Presenting with Gender Disorder', *Clinical Child Psychology and Psychiatry,* 2019, 24 (2) 338-352

[297] Tordoff, D. et al., 'Mental Health Outcomes in Transgender and Nonbinary Youths Receiving Gender-Affirming Care', *JAMA Network Open,* 2022, 5(2), e220978

[298] Warrier, V. et al., 'Elevated rates of autism, other neurodevelopmental and psychiatric diagnoses, and autistic traits in transgender and gender-diverse individuals', *Nature Communications,* 2020, vol. 11, Article 5869; Butwicka, A.

et al, 'Increased risk for substance use-related problems in autism spectrum disorders: a population-based cohort study', *Journal of Autism and Developmental Disorders,* 2017, 47(1), 80-89; Anderson, S.A.R. and Catallozzi, M., 'Autism Spectrum Disorder and the Risk of Substance Use Disorder. A Call for Targeted Screening and Prevention in Adolescents', *JAMA Pediatrics,* 2021, 175(2), e205376, doi:10.1001/jamapediatrics.2020.5376; Sizoo, B. et al., 'Treatment seeking adults with autism or ADHD and co-morbid substance use disorder: prevalence, risk factors and functional disability', Drug and Alcohol Dependence (Journal), 2010, 107(1), 44-50

[299] Rajkumar, R.P., 'Gender Identity Disorder and Schizophrenia...', op. cit.

[300] For the Bristol, North Somerset, South Gloucestershire Clinical Commissioning Group, North Bristol NHS Trust and Devon Partnership NHS Trust, see Humphries, W., 'Disputed trans guide gets NHS nod', 15.02.2020, *The Times*

[301] Dhejne, C. et al., 'Long-term follow-up of transsexual persons undergoing sex reassignment surgery: cohort study in Sweden', Scott, J. (ed.), *PLOS One,* 2011, 6(2), e16885

[302] De Vries, A.L. et al, 'Puberty suppression in adolescents with gender identity disorder: a prospective follow-up study', *Journal of Sexual Medicine,* 2011, 8, 2276-2283

[303] Davies-Arai, S., 'Is 'affirmation' an appropriate approach ...', Diagnostic and Statistical Manual of Mental Disorders, fifth edition, Arlington, VA, American Psychiatric Association, 2013; Kreukels, B.P. and Cohen-Kettenis, P.T., 'Puberty Suppression in Gender Identity Disorder: The Amsterdam Experience', National Review of Endocrinology, 2011, 17(7), 466-472; Zucker, K.J., 'Measurement of psychosexual differentiation', Archives of Sexual Behavior, 2005, 34(4), 375-388

[304] Steensma, T.D. et al., 'Desisting and persisting gender dysphoria after childhood: A qualitative follow-up study', *Clinical Child Psychology and Psychiatry,* 2011, 16(4), 499-516

[305] Shrier, A., 'Gender Activists Are Trying to Cancel My Book. Why is Silicon Valley Helping Them?' *Quillette,* 07.11.2020

[306] Lord (Robert) Winston quoted by Evans, M., 'Freedom to think: the need for thorough assessment and treatment of gender dysphoric children', *BJPsych Bulletin,* 2021, 45, 285-290

[307] Hunter, P.K., 'Political Issues Surrounding Gender-Affirming Care for Transgender Youth', *JAMA Pediatrics,* 2022, 176(3), 322-323, referring to: De Vries, A.L., 'Challenges in timing puberty suppression for gender-nonconforming adolescents', *Journal of Pediatrics,* 2020, 146(4).

[308] National Institute for Health and Care Excellence, 'Gonadotrophin releasing hormone analogues for children and adolescents with gender dysphoria', 11.03.2021

[309] Hunter, P.K., Political Issues Surrounding Gender-Affirming Care...', op. cit.

[310] Benjamin, C. et al., 'Political Issues Surrounding Gender-Affirming Care for Transgender Youth – Reply', *JAMA Pediatrics,* 2022, 176(3), 323

[311] Southem, K., 'Florida passes 'don't say gay' bill for schools in a victory for DeSantis', 09.03.2022, *The Times*

[312] Park, B.C., Das, R. K. and Drolet, B.C., 'Increasing criminalization of gender-affirming care for transgender youths — a politically motivated crisis', *JAMA Pediatrics,* published online 13.09.2021, doi:10.1001/jamapediatric, 2021.2969

[313] Tavistock and Portman NHS Foundation Trust Gender Identity Services Inspection Report, 20.01.2021

[314] Independent Review of Gender Identity Services for Children and Young People: Interim Report, cass.independent-review.uk, February 2022

[315] Evans, M., 'Freedom to think ...' op. cit, loc. cit.

[316] 'Banning Conversion Therapy', Response submitted ..., op. cit.

[317] White, D. 'Trans conversion therapy must be outlawed, Theresa May tells Johnson', The Times. 01.07.2022

[318] Milton, J., '4 bills in the Queen's Speech that could shape the future of LGBTQ+ rights in the UK', 10.02.2022, *Pink News*

[319] 'Disappointment on conversion therapy bans latest', News from BACP, 01.04.2022

[320] Milton, J., '4 bills in the Queen's Speech ...' op. cit.

[321] 'View on the collapse of the 'Safe to be Me' conference: Undone by Intolerance', 08.04.2022, *The Times*

[322] Wilcock, D., 'New row over conversion therapy 'ban' as No. 10 confirms law will still allow gay adults to consent to 'abhorrent' practice to try to alter their sexuality – while a fresh battle looms over transgender rights', 10.05.2022, *The Daily Mail*

323 'Banning Conversion Therapy', Presented to Parliament by the Secretary of State ...', op. cit.

324 Bannerman, L. 'Give irreversible gender drugs ...', op. cit.